Railway World SPECIAL

RAILS TO THE ISLES

FORT WILLIAM-MALLAIG

D1081197

Front cover:
No 44767 skirts the Western end of Loch Eilt with an SRPS excursion, 16 August 1986.
Dr W. A. Sharman

Back cover top:
After a sudden snow shower, No 5305 is prepared for 'West Highlander' duty at Fort William's Tom Na Faire depot; 29 March 1987. *Author*

Back cover bottom:
No 37085 heads the Corpach freight trip back towards Fort William, with a snow-covered Ben Nevis as a backdrop, 28 May 1986. *Author*

Right:
The driver of No 44767 takes the token for the 'Royal Scotsman' at Banavie in August 1986. The age of technology is taking shape alongside the original signal box in the form of the new Banavie Signalling Centre. *Author*

First published 1991

ISBN 0 7110 1978 9

Published by Ian Allan Ltd, Shepperton, Surrey; and printed by Ian Allan Printing Ltd at their works at Coombelands in Runnymede, England

Published by

IAN ALLAN LTD

Terminal House Shepperton TW17 8AS
Telephone: Walton-on-Thames (0932) 228950
Fax: 0932 232366   Telex: 929806 IALLAN G
Registered Office: Terminal House Shepperton TW17 8AS
Phototypeset and Printed by Ian Allan Printing at their works at
Coombelands in Runnymede, England

Contents

Introduction

Writing as a mere Englishman, whose first encounter with this magnificent Scottish Railway was on a Wirral Railway Circle 'Road to the Tales Isles' railtour in May 1975, and like many others as one who has only become better acquainted with the line since the introduction of a regular steam service in 1984, I feel something of a fraud. However, the successful return to steam traction has, via the media of tourist brochures, picture postcards, national television, numerous railway magazine articles and simply word of mouth, brought this former BR 'backwater' to the notice of railway enthusiasts, holidaymakers and the general public from all over Britain and indeed from further afield.

I have not set out to write a detailed or definitive history of the line, as this has already been extremely well done, as the bibliography appended to this work makes clear. What I have attempted to do

Right:
Deputising for 'K1' 2-6-0 No 2005 due to exceptionally high fire risk, No 37409 *Loch Awe* heads the 'Queen of Scots' luxury train across Glenfinnan viaduct, 4 May 1990. *Author*

Below:
The West Highland Extension Railway, Banavie Junction-Mallaig.

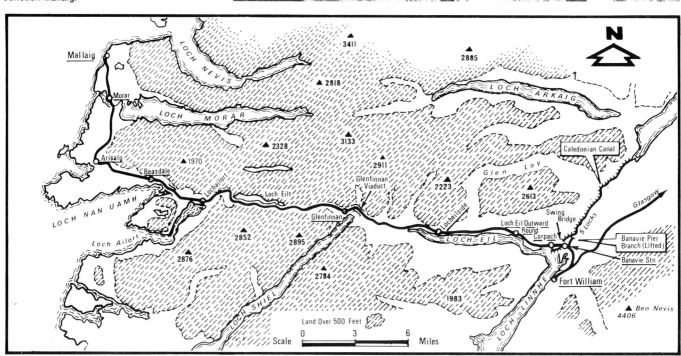

is to portray something of the atmosphere of this agreeable stretch of railway, both in terms of the men who worked the line in the days of steam and more recent operations. I have also included a glimpse – and, regrettably, it can be no more than that – of the behind-the-scenes activity that makes regular steam operation in the closing years of the 20th century a reality.

I have concluded with a look at the 'Mallaig Road' as part of the BR network, with a look at recent developments such as the introduction of 'Sprinter' units and the advent of radio signalling, plus an attempt to assess what the future has in store.

At the same time, I hope this volume will fill a gap in the railway bookshelf, in

Above:
No 5305 oozes atmosphere at Mallaig, 29 March 1987. *Author*

Above right:
Peace and tranquility alongside Loch Eil, May 1984. *Author*

the shape of a reasonably priced reminder of what has become, in recent years, one of the best known, and best loved, railways in Britain.

Much of the attraction of the railway lies in its magnificent setting, and consequently much of the 'feel' of the Mallaig Extension which I have tried to put across lies in the photographs. I must place on record my enormous debt of gratitude to so many of this country's leading railway photographers, who have

willingly parted with their priceless prints and transparencies to make this book possible.

I must also acknowledge the assistance of the many members of railway staff at all levels, both past and present, who have been willing to share their experiences with me. I would particularly like to thank Iain Cameron, David Lawrie, Bill Strachan, Elliot Ironside and Ronnie McLennan, without whose help this volume could not have been written.

Bob Avery
Carluke, Strathclyde
May 1990

Below:
Gradient profile.

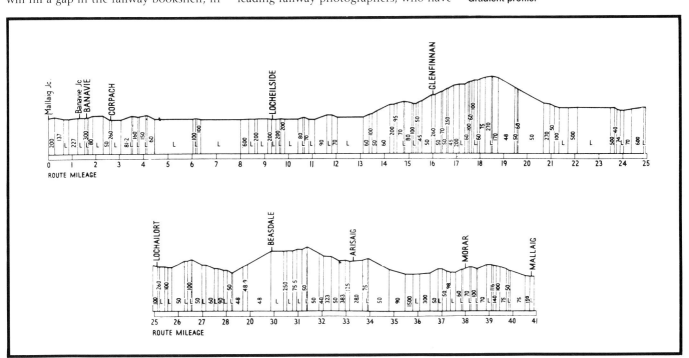

History and Background

If it were not for the midges, Glenfinnan station during the summer months would probably rank near the top of the list of the world's most idyllic railway stations. With a backdrop of gorse, pine, rhododendron and heather, and the nearby peaceful sound of running water, it is difficult to perceive this area of Lochaber without the railway, the parallel A830 road with its seemly endless process of foreign motor caravans bound for the Skye Ferry, and the coaches parked at the Glenfinnan Monument Visitor Centre.

Our imaginations can only attempt to conjure up an idea of what difficulties life must have held for the crofting and, further west, fishing communities before the coming of what was then modern technology in the shape of the West Highland Extension Railway in 1901.

It is important to realise that making life easier for the people of the far west of mainland Scotland was not the sole, or even the prime, motivation for extending the West Highland Railway westwards. Fort William as the terminus of the line from Glasgow had proved to be somewhat limiting. Although passenger trains during the summer were well loaded, those in the winter months often ran with barely a compartment full of travellers. Freight traffic was meagre and showed no signs of aspiring to the levels hoped for by the promotors. The productive fishing grounds off the West coast were a long way by sea from Fort William. A branch to the sea was what was needed.

The 'branch line' to Mallaig (which, before the coming of the railway, existed as no more than the tiniest of crofting communities) was planned to run from a connection with the Fort William-Banavie branch, and would be just under 40 miles in length. The intention was to capture for the West Highland (which was quickly absorbed into the North British Railway) a slice of the supposedly lucrative potential fish traffic, which had, thus far, failed to develop for want of a quick, reliable means of quickly transporting the fish to where it was wanted,

which was largely London and the South East.

The thinking of the directors of the company was no doubt influenced by the fact that the rival Highland Railway was in the process of extending its empire to Kyle of Lochalsh, on the West Coast some 30 miles north of Mallaig.

The construction of the railway was heavily dealyed while the appropriate

legislation went through parliament. Delaying tactics by the Highland Railway which, for obvious reasons, fiercely opposed the construction of the Mallaig line was one factor, but what really slowed things up was that the line's construction became a political handful of mud which was slung back and forth between Tory and Liberal sides of the House with considerable velocity.

Right:
Sir Robert McAlpine's innovative use of concrete for civil engineering has stood the test of time well. No 44932 crosses the River Morar, 12 August 1986. *Dr W. A Sharman*

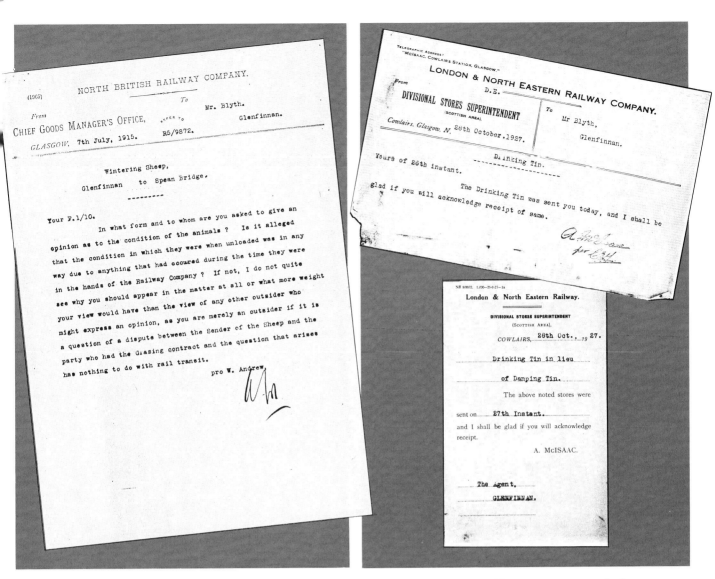

To cut a long story short, what it was really all about was that the line by itself was never expected fully to pay its way and that a subsidy of some sort would be required from the start. The ruling Tory party approved of transport being publicly subsidised but the Liberals in opposition did not. As is so often the case, personalities got involved and in the ensuing political battle, the real issue – the transport needs of the communities of Lochaber – were forgotten. That a new railway venture which required subsidy from the start should be considered by a Tory government seems remarkable in the political climate of today, but when one considers the complete absence of a practical alternative means of transport, the party line can perhaps be more readily understood if a comparison is made with the attitude prevailing in high places towards motorway construction in recent times.

Although the West Highland (Mallaig Extension) Act had been passed by Parliament on 31 July 1894, the antics of the elected representatives of the Scottish people succeeded in defeating the associated Guarantee Bill, without which construction could not start, and it was to be another two years before completion of the legislative requirements.

These delays meant that Messrs Lucas & Aird, the contractors who had build the West Highland 'proper' to Fort William, and had stayed on in the area in the hope of getting the Mallaig line contract, had upped and gone. The new contractors for the line were the Glasgow firm of Sir Robert McAlpine & Sons.

Sir Robert was a strong believer in the new building medium of mass concrete, and, as the local stone was not suitable for bridge building, he was able to make full use of the new material. Virtually all structures on the line, from the 21-arch curved Glenfinnan viaduct and the then innovative 127ft 6in single span over Borrodale Burn down to platforms and buildings are constructed of concrete, as are the harbour walls at Mallaig. Sir Robert gained the nickname 'Concrete Bob', which was first applied as a derisory term by those contractors who still favoured the use of iron. But concrete was considerably cheaper to construct, did not rust and did not require painting and the Mallaig line had to be built cheaply. The nickname has stuck and the fact that it is considered complimentary in recognition of Sir Robert's pioneering use of the medium has been evidenced by a ceremony at Glenfinnan in 1986, at which one of Eastfield (Glasgow) Depot's regular West Highland locomotives, No 37425, (since transferred elsewhere) has been named *Concrete Bob* on one side and *Sir Robert McAlpine* on the other.

Sir Robert's son, who was another Robert, spearheaded the development of a technique for using water (of which there was – and still is – a plentiful supply) to drive turbines to provide compressed air for the drills to cut their way through the extremely hard rock to make the numerous cuttings and 11 tunnels, the longest of which is Borrodale tunnel at 350yd. The alterntative would have been steam driven compressors which were considerably less powerful and slower.

But despite these innovations, progress was chronically hampered by shortage of staff. Although facilities provided for the 3,500 navvies were by the standards of the day, excellent, the McAlpines had great difficulty in retaining skilled labour. The long distance from home, and the often wet and cold weather were no doubt contributory factors.

Probably the most famous piece of folklore connected with the construction of the line concerns an incident which took place during the building of Glenfinnan Viaduct. It is said that a horse and cart, engaged in the transportation of materials on to the viaduct, fell into the hollow interior of one of the concrete pillars. Because of the difficult and costly recovery operation that would have been necessary, the remains of the beast and cart rest inside the viaduct to this day.

The line finally opened to passenger traffic on 1 April 1901. The effect on the communities it served was dramatic. Fort William was now within the scope of a day's return travel, frequency of public transport was quadrupled and the fare was slashed. As expected, fish traffic from the railway-owned harbour at Mallaig, dominated operations there. Although the line never paid its way, contributions from the taxpayers' kitty were not as high as had originally been feared.

Right:
Glenfinnan was unlikely to be involved in the transport of bananas, but was in receipt of company circulars on the subject nevertheless.
Glenfinnan Station Museum Trust

Far right:
Today the mind boggles at the thought of dead animals being conveyed by rail, but in 1908 it was obviously routine enough for the North British to print pro-formas for correspondence.
Glenfinnan Station Museum Trust

Left:
Are there remains of a horse and cart inside these concrete piers? No 44767, Glenfinnan Viaduct, July 1986. *Author*

Below:
An undated photograph of Mallaig, but obviously taken very soon after the line's opening. The concrete edges of the platform still look new and untarnished. The locomotive on the left is 'West Highland Bogie' 4-4-0 No 346, and that on the right is a Class 'C' 0-6-0 in its original form. Note the magnificent clerestory stock, and the fact that most of the town's buildings have yet to be built.
Locomotive Publishing Company

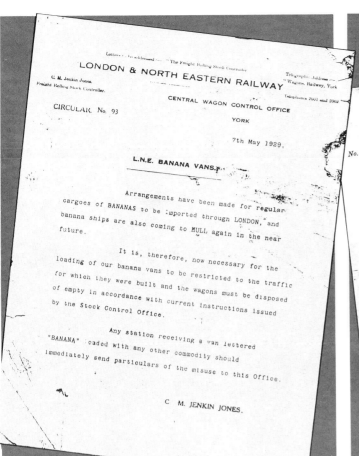

Letters to be addressed — "The Freight Rolling Stock Controller.

LONDON & NORTH EASTERN RAILWAY

C. M. Jenkin Jones,
Freight Rolling Stock Controller.

Telegraphic Address —
"Wagons, Railway, York

Telephones 2001 and 2002

CENTRAL WAGON CONTROL OFFICE

YORK

CIRCULAR No. 93

7th May 1929,

L.N.E. BANANA VANS.

Arrangements have been made for regular cargoes of BANANAS to be imported through LONDON, and banana ships are also coming to HULL again in the near future.

It is, therefore, now necessary for the loading of our banana vans to be restricted to the traffic for which they were built and the wagons must be disposed of empty in accordance with current instructions issued by the Stock Control Office.

Any station receiving a van lettered "BANANA" loaded with any other commodity should immediately send particulars of the misuse to this Office.

C. M. JENKIN JONES.

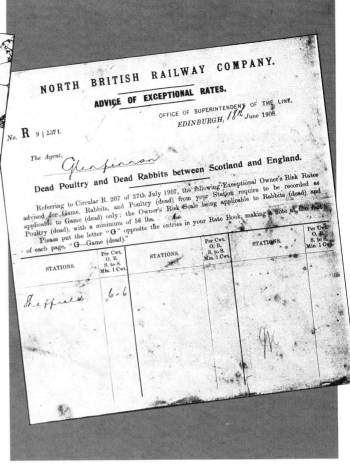

NORTH BRITISH RAILWAY COMPANY.

ADVICE OF EXCEPTIONAL RATES.

OFFICE OF SUPERINTENDENT OF THE LINE,
EDINBURGH, 18th June 1908.

No. R 9/2071.

The Agent, Glenfinnan

Dead Poultry and Dead Rabbits between Scotland and England.

Referring to Circular R. 207 of 27th July 1907, the following Exceptional Owner's Risk Rates advised for Game, Rabbits, and Poultry (dead) from your Station require to be recorded as applicable to Game (dead) only; the Owner's Risk Scale being applicable to Rabbits (dead) and Poultry (dead), with a minimum of 56 lbs.

Please put the letter "G" opposite the entries in your Rate Book, making a note at the foot of each page, "G—Game (dead)."

STATIONS.	Per Cwt. O. R. S. to S. Min. 1 Cwt.	STATIONS.	Per Cwt. O. R. S. to S. Min. 1 Cwt.	STATIONS.	Per Cwt. O. R. S. to S. Min. 1 Cwt.
Sheffield	6·6				

Locomotives and Footplate Life

The Mallaig extension differs from the West Highland 'main line' south from Fort William in that while the Glasgow line demands locomotives which can slog upgrade for long climbs, the 'Road to the Isles' consists of a series of short, vicious gradients with very sharp curves. Loads were not heavy by standards adopted on trunk routes through more conventional terrain, though the gradients and curvature encountered on the whole West Highland network will tax any locomotive venturing north of Craigendoran Junction to the limit, and this still holds true with today's Class 37 diesels.

The first locomotives regularly to work the Mallaig extension were Reid's 'West Highland Bogie' 4-4-0s, which were basically a standard North British 4-4-0 with a shortened wheelbase and smaller driving wheels. Eighteen of these engines were built between 1893 and 1896, though not all worked the West Highland. As well as the 4-4-0s, freight workings were in the hands of Holmes 'C'

Class 0-6-0s. These became LNER Class 'J36', and were associated with Fort William until the end of steam working in the early 1960s. Furthermore, as described elsewhere in this volume, preserved Class 'C' No 673 *Maude* made a dramatic return to the Mallaig line in 1984.

All the West Highland bogies had gone to the scrapyard by 1924, except No 695, which was modified with superheater and large cylinders, and continued to work between Glasgow and Mallaig until 1943.

Reid's intermediate 'K' Class 4-4-0 (LNER Class 'D32') and 'B' Class 0-6-0 (LNER Class 'J37') were introduced in 1906, and became regular performers on all parts of the West Highland network. In 1913 another Reid design, his 'Glen' 4-4-0, appeared. They were not intended specifically for West Highland duties, but most, if not all, members of the class appeared in Lochaber at some time in their careers, and consequently the class

became synonymous with the West Highland. From their introduction they took the main passenger turns, and appeared regularly on the Mallaig extension, though were rather more common between Fort William and Glasgow. No 256 *Glen Douglas* survives, stuffed and mounted in Glasgow's Museum of Transport in the Kelvin Hall.

In the mid-1930s the 'Glens' were replaced on the Mallaig extension by the new 'K2' 2-6-0s, which were the first engines of LNER, rather than North British, design to work the line. Sir Nigel Gresley's 'K2s' were to be the staple motive power of the line for over 25 years. All were named after lochs, and could take 40 tons more than a 'Glen', which meant that the usual string of fish

Below:
Ex-NBR 'Glen' 4-4-0 No 9405 *Glen Spean* at Mallaig on 19 June 1937, waiting to leave with a Fort William train. The steam cranes for working on the quayside lines are clearly visible.
H. C. Casserley

Right:
The original Fort William station on 14 June 1927. 'Glen' 4-4-0 *Glen Shiel* eventually became BR No 62479. No trace of the station remains today, as it was demolished to make way for the town centre bypass road along the edge of Loch Linnhe. *H. C. Casserley*

vans could be attached to a Fort William bound train without the need for a pilot engine.

There was a need for a still more powerful engine, particularly on the line south from Fort William, and Gresley turned his attention to providing something specifically for the West Highland. The result was another, larger, 2-6-0, – the 'K4'. Six 'K4s' were built altogether, and all but abolished the need to double head heavy passenger trains to Glasgow. Because through Glasgow-Mallaig trains had to reverse at Fort William, 'K4s' made only occasional forays on to the Mallaig line, with most through trains from Glasgow going forward behind a 'K2'. 'K4' No 3442's return to Mallaig in 1989 is described elsewhere in this volume.

'K4' No 3445 *MacCailin Mor* was rebuilt by Edward Thompson at Doncaster in 1945. It emerged as Class 'K1/1', with two cylinders (the 'K4s' had three) and increased boiler pressure. It became the prototype for another class which became associated with the Mallaig line, the 'K1' mixed traffic 2-6-0, which first emerged after Nationalisation in 1949. Six of the class were Mallaig line regulars, and supplemented the ageing 'K2s'. LMS 'Black Fives' began to appear between Glasgow and Fort William, but never appeared on the Mallaig line. Four ex-LMS Ivatt 2-6-0s were introduced in the spring of 1953, but were not a success, only lasting until June. In the early 1960s BR Standard Class '4' 2-6-0 No 76001 made regular appearances on the line.

Mention must also be made of the two Gresley 'V4' 2-6-2s, No 61700 *Bantam Cock*, and unnamed No 61701, known as 'Bantam Hen' by loco crews. Though intended as a general mixed traffic type for the whole LNER system, in fact only these two were built, and spent the majority of their lives working from Eastfield, including freight and passenger turns as far as Mallaig, though the turntable at Mallaig had to be modified so that a 'V4' could be accommodated. 'B1' 4-6-0s also started in the early years of the 1960s, and Mallaig's turntable was further modified to take the increased length.

There was a complement of eight sets of locomen at Mallaig, which was strengthened to nine during the summer.

Centre right:
Holmes Class 'C' (J36) 0-6-0 No 9764 on Fort William shed, 14 June 1927. *H. C. Casserley*

Right:
LNER 'K2' 2-6-0 No 4692 *Loch Eil* enters Mallaig with a train from Fort William, 19 June 1937. *H. C. Casserley*

In addition there were six cleaners, two steam crane drivers, and one 'guy for shovelling ashes' who acted as relief crane driver.

There was plenty of opportunity for cleaners to gain firing experience. One such turn is recalled: '. . . It was pitch black. We went to Glenfinnan. I didn't know where I was, I was just shovelling coal. I'd never been past Morar on an engine before. We were piloting a fish special, and we ran back to Mallaig tender first.'

This was one of the few occasions where tender first running took place on the West Highland. A fish train which was overweight for a Mallaig 'K2' would take a pilot engine – probably another 'K2' – as far as Glenfinnan. At Glenfinnan the option was either to continue forward to Fort William to turn, or to run back to Mallaig tender first. What of the present arrangement where the preserved engine runs back to Fort William tender first? 'There'd have been a riot if they'd asked us to do that.'

'I remember being passed out for driving by Inspector Bartholomew from Fort William. We had a 'K2' with 220 tons, four coaches and 10 fish, which was right up to a full load. We had 125 of steam and the water was only so high in the glass. We left a minute late and arrived in Fort William a minute late, and Bartholomew stood behind me all the way.

'After that there was a written exam. There were six of us altogether, three from Mallaig and three from The Fort. We were doing our exam when one of the Fort William men burst in and said to Bartholomew, "When are we on?" Bartholomew told him, "When I want you I'll send for you." He was the only one who failed.'

At Mallaig there were six 'K2s'. The four senior drivers had regular firemen, and took their own locomotives wherever possible.

'Seventeen Eighty Nine (61789) was Colin MacLean's engine, and Hugh Mac-Beth was his fireman. Willie Letham had Seventeen Eighty Two. Eighty Three was that little bit more powerful than the others. They all came and went, and were usually fine when they'd been to Cowlairs. But Eighty Three was the best. She wouldn't take a heavy fire like the rest of them – she'd steam better with a light fire.

'Big Alistair Mackenzie weighed 18 stone and was built accordingly. He'd been at Eastfield for 20 years and came back to Mallaig where he was born and bred. He was so big he had to ease himself on to the engine. He only knew one way to go – with the regulator wide open!

'He was a great mate altogether, but you had to know how to fire to him. If you didn't have a decent fire leaving Mallaig you were struggling – the fire would be coming out of the door!

'There was a fireman called Douggie McDougall, who asked me for a change of shifts. He was Early Passenger, and I was 11 o'clock spare. We were coming back at Lochailort, and we were to pass an up fish special, and it was Big Alistair and Douggie. Alistair used to creep into stations, but once he'd got the token, the regulator was open and he'd be away! As he left Lochailort you should have seen the sparks fly! Douggie said to me a few days later, "How d'you keep steam to that man?"

'He was great to fire to, but was very pig headed. We used to have long discussions about all sorts of things. I'd have one view and he'd have the other. Once I was so sure I was right I went home and got an encyclopedia. The next day I took it along and showed him. He read the bit in the book and looked at me. "That'd be wrong", he said.

'He was never in a hurry. We were working the morning goods back from Fort William and I had an engagement in the afternoon. I asked him to get back as quickly as possible. Before the one o'clock left. "Ay, We'll see" he said. We met the one o'clock at Lochailort.'

Although Mallaig men spent most of their time on 'K2s', they occasionally saw other engines, in particular 'K4s' and the

Left:
***Loch Eil** again, this time as BR No 61782, at Mallaig on 22 April 1952. The points immediately behind the tender were the cause of the derailment referred to when the weighted point lever was released too soon.* *H. C. Casserley*

two 'V4' 'Bantam Cocks'. Opinion varied about the 'K4s'. 'I always seemed to struggle for steam with a 'K4' – I must have been firing it wrong. I never fancied them – the injectors were awful heavy.' Conversely, 'Once I was with Archie MacBeth on the 12.30 passenger. We had a "K4" with eight coaches, and steam was just no problem at all'.

The 'V4s' demanded a special firing technique owing to a rather short firebox. 'You had to wear gloves, to get the coal round the corner.' An incident was recalled with a 'K4' which lost her middle cylinder on to the track on Glenfinnan viaduct. It was the day of Glenfinnan Highland Games, and considerable disruption to the timetable, which included specials from Fort William, resulted. There was an instruction to footplatemen working on K4s that regular checks had to be made on a crucial lock nut on the centre cylinder, though whether or not this was a result of the Glenfinnan incident is not clear.

The nature of the workload at Mallaig meant that a driver's most important attribute was his route knowledge, and because of the single route worked by Mallaig drivers, an in-depth appreciation of every yard of the Mallaig extension was quickly obtained. 'We never got lost, and I could find my way about even in pitch black. Even if I fell asleep I'd know where I was. I remember once I'd been playing badminton at Fort William, and was travelling home on the last passenger. My friends asked "Where are we now?" In the darkness, I was able to reply, "Oh, we're just by McPhee's house." They were astonished, but I was right.' (McPhee was a surfaceman who lived in an isolated cottage near the line alongside the southern shore of Loch Eilt. The derelict remains of the cottage are still clearly visible).

'The fastest I ever did the return trip was under an hour both ways, with Freddie Watson. I can't remember the engine. It was a fish special and back with empty vans. I was playing football that evening and desperate to get back. On the way back there was one of those new "Insulfish" vans in the train. As we ran into

Mallaig I looked back and saw it was on fire, but we never stopped for it – I just needed to get back! Geordie Hector was in the booking office, and he was playing in the same team. As I was booking off in the shed, Geordie was 'phoning Arisaig to ask if there was any word of the return "fish". (The booked time was 1hr and 40 min.)

'It was usual for the lunchtime passenger to get 20-25min late start attaching fish vans. The agent (stationmaster) would come up to the engine and say "do your best" which meant we'd to try and make up time, so as he could record less delay than had actually taken place. Sometimes we could make up 20min to Fort William. Nowadays if you made up 3min you'd get a 'please explain'.

'Cleaning the engines was a hell of a job. You'd clean an engine for 5hr and make it look spick and span. After one run to Fort William, you'd think it hadn't been cleaned for a fortnight. It was hopeless. After I came back from National Service in 1952 they asked me, "What are you going to do?"

"Clean engines," I replied. Clean engines? What kind of a job is that? It was the only time I really felt like leaving the railway. But we got plenty of firing turns, usually on fish specials.'

One Mallaig driver was married to a lady who was involved in the running of Mallaig's Marine Hotel, and would regularly assist behind the bar, and with other duties in the hotel. 'I was serving lunch, and a customer told me he hadn't time for a dessert as he had to catch the one o'clock passenger. I told him he'd plenty of time, and served his sweet. I could see from the hotel that the Skye ferry hadn't yet arrived, so I knew we'd get a late start. You should have seen his face when he saw me walking down the platform to the engine!'

The sense of teamwork which existed in a small community such as Mallaig meant that if Railway Operations went slightly wrong, resulting, for example, in a minor derailment, then it was all hands to the pumps to correct matters before news 'leaked out' and resulted in forms to be filled in, reports to be written, inquiries and Head Office investigations. In the loco depot a short siding ended without a buffer stop, just a redundant sleeper placed across the rails. One day a rough shunt knocked a coal wagon over the end. 'The coal just bounced in the wagon. Both the steam cranes were cold,

Left:
'K2' No 4698 (later BR 61788) ***Loch Rannoch*** *with a Glasgow-Mallaig train at Morar, in the summer of 1939.* *The late C. Hamilton Ellis*

so we uncoupled the rest of the wagons, went back with the engine and pulled the wagon back on. For years afterwards you could see the marks in the concrete where the flanges had sunk in.

'When you were a small boy in Mallaig one of the great things to do was to go down to the railway and ride up and down on the pilot engine. It wasn't a pilot as such – just one of the "K2s". As the years went on, everbody did it. I remember one lad on with me – he's the skipper of his own boat now. It was three or four o'clock in the afternoon, and it was a "K2". We ran on to the turntable. We were pushing the thing round, and the engine ran backwards off the table. It was the tender. The first axle was off, the second axle was just off but no more. If we'd have gone forwards we'd have crashed through the bothy. I said to young Cameron, "Get away from here as quick as you can!" They blamed it on the vacuum brake on the "K2" but it was him, he'd been messing about. I know it was a "K2" because it had a reversing lever instead of the screw on a "K1". Alec Jack (another Mallaig driver) said to me "You'd better have a go at getting it on." This meant as we were half way round I'd about six or seven feet to get the engine on and stop. We managed it. It was another of those escapades that nobody knew about. Nowadays you'd have to have fitters, tool vans and all that. Mind you, you can't just lift a diesel up like that.

'I remember the points leading up to the coal stage, there was a ball (weight) on the lever to hold the points over. Me and my pal, we were just cleaners at the time, and we were letting an engine off the shed. My pal let go of the ball as soon as the cab railings had passed him, and of course the tender went off the road. Alec Jack was the driver and he said "Right, we'll have a go at getting it on." But every time we tried, the tender just

Above:
One of the two Gresley 'V4' 2-6-2s, No 1700 *Bantam Cock* is seen on a Fort Wiliam-bound freight near Crianlarich, during the last years of the LNER company's existence.
The late P. Ransome-Wallis

bounced over the sleepers. I don't know how many sleepers and chairs we wrecked. But we couldn't get it on, so there was a wee bit of an enquiry about that.

Below:
A works portrait of 'K4' No 3441 (later BR 61993) *Loch Long*. *Real Photographs*

'I remember another tale about Alec Jack. We'd worked to Fort William with a "K2", and when we got there they took the engine off us, and we'd to wait for an engine to bring back. We went down to the Pier Hotel. Alec knew everybody – he used to drive on the Fort Augustus branch before he came to Mallaig. He had quite a few drinks – I was just a youngster and didn't bother. Eventually we got an engine and came back light. It was a Friday night, and all I wanted was to get back, washed and out. I remember coming past the croft at Morar and Alec was hanging out of the cab window, as drunk as a lord! I was trying to get every-

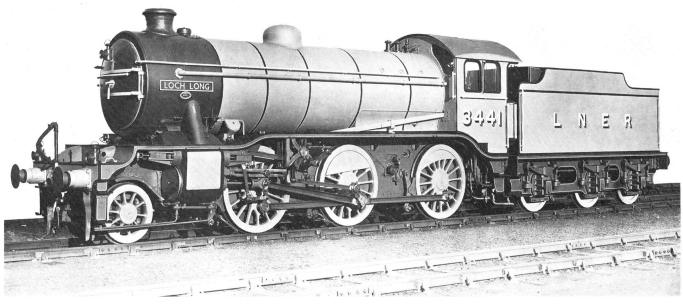

thing organised – boiler full, fire dropped and off. I thought the road would be set for us onto the shed, but we ran on to one of the pier lines and – Bang! We hit a row of vans and the first two or three came off the road. The shed chargeman came over, and the crane driver, and they put them back on for us. No one ever made out a report. Everything was fine after that. End of story.

'Alec was a great driver. I used to reckon that I shovelled less coal than most people because of the way he drove. He didn't like the diesels – he used to let me drive them. Unfortunately he died suddenly in his house on a Saturday night. (A run from Mallaig to Fort William with driver Jack is described in detail in O. S. Nock's book *British Railways From The Footplate* published by Ian Allan in 1950.)

'One day Willie Letham and Big John McKechnie were talking about what the future held in store. "Wouldn't it be great," I remember Willie saying, "if we could earn £1,000 a year? And won't it be great when the diesels come – we won't have to do any work!" John McKechnie stayed in a lineside house just beyond Morar. "Ay," he said, "but what'll we do for coal?" (In common with most houses near the line, domestic coal was unoffically provided free by throwing large lumps off passing locomotives.)

'Once I was with Jock Haggerty, and a passenger came up at Mallaig and asked if he could come on the footplate. He was an American railway nut and wore some kind of pin-striped boiler suit. His wife stayed in the coaches. Anyway, we had a terrible trip, short of steam and the rails were bad, and the gauge glass was broken so there was steam everywhere – typical, just when we had a visitor. As we dropped away from Glenfinnan, Jock said to him, "There's Prince Charlie's monument." "Who's Prince Charlie?" asked the American. There followed a short history lesson. When it was over he said, "There's one thing I can never understand about you Goddam Scots – when you're not fighting somebody else, you're fighting amongst your Goddam selves!" He turned out to be the Mayor of somewhere in New Jersey!

'When the spray came over the track I've known us take an hour and a half to Morar with slipping. Sometimes it was so bad the signalman would let us out on the pilot after the train had cleared the points, and we'd catch up and shove him up to Morar. There was nothing about that in the Rules and Regulations, but he'd never have made it on his own.

'One Christmastime we went out with Jackie McLelland on an engine to get some holly. He was awful frightened because we hadn't got a tablet. But the passenger wasn't due till 12, and we'd to be back by half past 11. He was terrified, but we got his holly. I wasn't too bothered, I was only the fireman. The responsibility was his.

'I remember the very first diesel train into Mallaig. The Duchess of Kent had been to name a lifeboat, and we'd had to clear the quay of wagons. We were putting them back, and an officers' special full of dignitaries was on its way with a diesel. The signalman had let us onto the main line to do a shunt. Three of the vans dropped off the road, fouling the main line. The steam crane had finished but still had a bit of steam left. The sig-

Below:
'K2' No 61789 *Loch Laidon* approaches Banavie with the afternoon empty fish vans for Mallaig on 16 June 1951, with snow still lying in the sheltered corries of Ben Nevis. The North British lattice post signal has no ladder, and is equipped with a pulley arrangement for tending to the signal lamp. *E. D. Bruton*

Above:
'J36' 0-6-0 No 65313 shunts stock at Fort William in 1963. The leading vehicle is the former 'Coronation Scot' observation coach which was used on Fort William-Glasgow workings. This site is now occupied by the dual carriageway Fort William town centre bypass road. *Eric Aitchison*

nalman should have blocked the line, but he took the big wigs special in and shouted "Quick, get them on!" The three of us and the crane driver have never moved so fast. We got the last one on and shunted clear just as the special came in round the corner, and no one ever knew.'

The diesels came in the early 1960s. The first diesel class to appear was the Birmingham Railway Carriage and Wagon Company's Sulzer-engined 1,250hp Type 2 Bo-Bo numbered from D5347 onwards, later to become Class 27. These engines, all of which were Scottish-based, became the staple power of the West Highland network until being ousted by the more powerful English Electric Type 3 Co-Co, which became Class 37. The other diesel class associated with the line was the NBL-Paxman 1,350hp Bo-Bo, ultimately Class 29, which appeared in the mid to late 1960s, until the withdrawal of the whole class

with technical problems in the early 1970s.

Other classes which put in occasional appearances were the ubiquitous BR-Sulzer Class 25s and the single-cabbed English Electric 1,000hp Class 20, known by drivers as 'thousands'. These latter classes appeared mainly on Fort William-Corpach trip freights, though occasionally appeared on passenger duties

Below:
'K2' No 61790 *Loch Lomond* alongside Loch Eil with a Mallaig-Fort William train.
The late Eric Treacy

deputising for Class 27 or 37 failures. Despite the coming of the diesel age, drivers still found that an intimate route knowledge was required. In particular, a driver could tell if all was not well by sound.

We were working to the Fort on a 27. As we crossed the viaduct (Glenfinnan) I said to my mate, did you hear that? We went on to the Fort and on the way back I heard it again. There had been no other trains since our last run to Fort William, but the Glasgow was in Glenfinnan up platform. I told the signalman to keep him there, and we phoned Fort William. The men on the Glasgow were cursing me upside down. When the Permanent Way arrived, they found a length of rail about a foot long had broken away, and it was the check rail that was holding us on.

'Another time we were coming back from Fort William. We'd just passed the end of Loch Eil. We'd had a great deal of rain and there was a wee bridge over a raging burn. When we got to Glenfinnan they told us the bridge had collapsed after we'd crossed it.

'Once we had a 27 which failed on a Fort William train around the back of Loch Eilt. (This spot, though clearly visible from the road, is one of the most inaccessible on the line.) I looked in the engine room and it was a burst pipe or something, there was no hope. My mate set off with the token towards Glenfinnan, and I thought, he's got a two-hour walk ahead of him. Some anglers in a boat came over and asked if there was a problem. They took him (the secondman with the token) across the loch in their boat. Just then the local p-way van came along – they'd set off from Glenfinnan to see where we were. They took him to Glenfinnan with the tablet. They took the engine off a down train at Glenfinnan, and we were only 35min late into the Fort. I thought we'd have been there all week.'

Another story is told about the last train from Fort William failing at Beasdale on a Saturday evening. As the train had proceeded along the line, the various signalboxes had switched out of circuit and the signalmen had gone home. It was thus impossible to admit an assisting engine from Fort William, and there wasn't one at Mallaig. This left no option but to accommodate the passengers in a nearby Hotel for the night, most travellers being locals who were delighted with this arrangement!

After the day's train service had ended, if there was a loco at Mallaig it was not unknown for as many people as possible to cram into the cab for a run to Morar, if there was a Ceilidh or other function going on. No doubt the same method of transport was laid on for the return journey!

There is absolutely no doubt that the events and tales related in this chapter represent but a minute proportion of available folklore, which one day may appear on bookshelves in a volume on their own. Although the Motive Power Department was the most glamorous in terms of popular appeal, it was only part of the overall picture. A railway cannot function with locomotives alone, and in the following chapter I have attempted to portray some of the atmosphere of other aspects of railway life in the West Highlands.

Life Off The Footplate

The fishing village of Mallaig as it stands today did not exist before the coming of the railway just after the turn of the century. As such it is not a 'typical' West Highland community, as its population is a mixed bag made up of families of fishermen from Scotland's north-east coast, bringing with them the necessary expertise to run the town's newly formed fishing industry, and also immigrants from Skye who came to Mallaig simply to find work – always a scarce commodity on the island. As such Mallaig grew up as a railway town. The influence of the railway Company went beyond the running of trains, and included the maintenance and running of the harbour, and the provision of the town's water supply. As late as 1952-3 – well into BR days, the Mallaig stationmaster's duties included reading water meters in various industrial premises, usually 'kippering sheds' where the freshly caught herring were smoked. In addition, the stationmaster was responsible for ensuring that the small lighthouse at the entrance to the harbour was kept topped up with paraffin, and a small rowing boat was provided for this purpose. In the early 1950s about 98% of available fish traffic was carried by rail, and any strange motor vehicle seen in the harbour area was swiftly sent packing by the stationmaster.

Although white fish was caught all the year round, providing a staple diet of freight traffic, the railway's busiest time was from the turn of the year to mid-March, which was the herring season. During this period, Mallaig's population would swell by a factor of four or five – not just additional fishermen but women who cleaned and prepared the fish, and men for packing.

'There were 13 places doing Kippers. They all employed 15-30 women, who would come to loco crews for hot water and coal. If they asked for coal we just gave it to them, and we could have as many kippers as we wanted. The women lived in very frugal surroundings – we called it Chinatown.'

Even the Salvation Army arrived to look after the spiritual needs of the town's floating population. The sudden influx of humanity – and their departure at the end of the herring season – meant special trains to and from distant parts, as many of the town's temporary residents spent their working lives travelling to whichever part of the country yielded the best catch. This usually meant North-East Scotland from May to September, East Anglia in the autumn, and Mallaig from Christmas to Eastertime.

Not surprisingly living and working conditions in the town were dreadful, and for the early part of the year Mallaig resembled a large Shanty town. It was said, with a fair degree of accuracy, that fishermen either died of religion or alcoholic poisoning, or sometimes both.

The four most important members of the community in Mallaig were the local Minister, Schoolteacher, Policeman and Stationmaster, and any newcomer was

Above left:
'K1' No 62052 pilots BR Standard 2-6-0 No 76001 on the approach to Glenfinnan with the 05.10 Glasgow Queen St-Mallaig on 17 July 1961.
Douglas Hume

Left:
'K1's Nos 62012 and 62011 double-head the 13.05 Mallaig-Glasgow on 26 August 1961. The train has just left the short twin tunnels at the top of the climb past Loch Eillt, and will now drift down to the station stop at Glenfinnan.
A. R. Butcher

Above:
The prototype 'K1/1' No 61997, *MacCailin Mor*
leaves Glenfinnan with the 13.00 Mallaig-Glasgow
during March 1956. *J. M. Jarvis/Colour-Rail*

Right:
NBL Type 2 diesel No D6103 leaves the original
Fort William station with a Mallaig train.
The late Derek Cross/Colour-Rail

Below right:
Fort William station on 30 May 1963. BRCW
Type 2 No D5352 awaits departure with the 09.55
to Mallaig. An unidentified sister engine arrives in
the background with the 07.25 from Mallaig.
John Marson

liable to be treated with suspicion until it could be proved that he could 'fit in'. This was particularly true in the case of the stationmaster. Whereas a stationmaster with a fishing community background, say, from north-east Scotland, would probably settle in without difficulty, a 'townie' from Glasgow might not fit in too well. The tale is told of a new stationmaster named Fairweather who was not over-popular. He married the local district nurse, who had come to Mallaig from the Isle of Skye. His railway colleagues arranged for a telegram to be sent to him on his wedding day. The telegram read, 'The forecast is unsettled but tonight there will be Fairweather over the Hebrides.' Mr Fairweather lasted just over a year on the West Highland.

The stationmaster's day started early, before 06.00, when the fish sales started on the quayside. The stationmaster had to know the fish merchant's business, and balance orders for empty vans with likely available traffic. Ten loaded fish vans could be attached to the 07.42 train to Fort William, and if there were more than this then a special had to be run, which had to leave ahead of the 07.42 to ensure connections south from Fort William. A decision had to be made as to whether a Fish Special was required, and this decision would be based on what was happening on the quayside. If one particular merchant bought herring, the stationmaster had to know, for example, whether or not these were likely to be sent for kippering or be required to be transported away by rail, in time for a 07.42 or earlier departure.

Mallaig men were hard workers and there was rarely any problem in getting staff to work overtime. However the pubs closed at 9pm, and it was a local 'agreement' that quayside porters and other railway staff would be allowed away between eight and nine. As long as the nightly skinful could be consumed, all was well and co-operation was assured. Whether or not a stationmaster was prepared to accept this was an indication of whether or not he would be accepted by his staff, and was one of the factors in the downfall of the aforementioned Mr Fairweather, whose idea of good staff relations was to invite staff to his home in the evenings to go through the rule book.

Accommodation for railway staff at Mallaig was available in the Hostel which was run by the locomotive department. A resident of the hostel fared better than many of the town's workforce, as he had hot water on tap, a cooked breakfast and lunch provided, a single room and 'some rare Ceildihs' in the evening, all for 1/– per night. As relief staff were on 7/6 per night expenses, this usually meant a net weekly profit of over £1.

The hostel was run by Mrs McGilvray whose husband drove the steam cranes on the quayside and was steam raiser at Mallaig shed. Mrs McGilvray kept a flock of chickens who ran freely round the station and its environs. The first up train, the 06.30 from Mallaig, was timetabled as a mixed, and, as well as a coach for the schoolchildren, conveyed empty coal wagons and a van for sundries such as empty gas cylinders and other miscellaneous items. One morning the stationmaster at Banavie had a few odds and ends to load into this van. On opening the doors, he was rather taken aback when several hens ran out on to the platform! After a short delay the itinerant birds were rounded up and put back into the van, and arrangements were made for the van to be returned to Mallaig later the same day.

Moving now to the other end of the line, Locheilside halt was in the care of a spinster, Flora McDonald, who lived in the station house with her sister, and kept the station extremely clean. Some of the surrounding estates belonged to Messrs WD & HO Wills, the tobacco giants. On these estates was bred a particular specialised breed of calf, and every so often there was a requirement to send one off to market at Carlisle, usually in a cattle wagon attached to the 06.30 mixed. The calves were very young and barely weaned, and one particular beast displayed a particularly wild temperament, where, as well as doing what comes naturally all over Miss McDonald's spotless platform, it ran off into the hills, where, as far as we know, it roams still.

The permanent way staff, or 'surfacemen', were a race apart. Most would per-

Below:
**Mallaig Driver Ewan MacDonald at the controls of
a Class 27 diesel.** *A. A. Vickers*

form any additional duties asked of them provided they could do it in their own time, as this was when most of their duties were done. A trait still common to West Highland railwayman (and, indeed, to many railwaymen) is that of a secondary part-time business interest. In Lochaber this was often crofting, and if a surfaceman lived near the railway his time could be evenly divided between looking after the track and fences and tending his own land and livestock. This system worked well as long as nobody tried to lay down that the specified hours should be adhered to.

The stationmaster at Banavie received each year a claim from a local crofter for sheep killed by trains. Whether the claim was met is not recorded, as the crofter in question was the ganger responsible for maintaining the fences on that particular stretch of line! Another favourite trick was to put the body of a sheep which had

died of natural causes on the rail line, thereby producing evidence of being hit by a train if anybody decided to investigate the claim.

The signalbox at Annat which controls the level crossing access to the Corpach pulp mill was built during WW2, when Corpach was an important naval base. The box survives today solely to control the crossing and its associated signals – the line's last semaphores. During the mid-1950s the box was manned by a widow crossing keeper who was 'paid in sweeties' for performing her duties faultlessly from dawn till dusk seven days a week. Nearby at Camus-Na-Ha was a crossing loop installed during the war to increase capacity of the line. The locking and signalling arrangements did not permit the crossing of passenger trains, although that's not to say that this was never done if it was thought that no-one was looking.

Above:
The 17.42 Mallaig-Fort William near Lochailort behind 'K1' No 62034, 14 May 1958.
I. S. Pearsall

Corpach station is situated at the Western entrance to the Caledonian Canal, and there were usually several boats moored in the basin. The station was manned by porters on alternate shifts, one of whom was Angus McDonald, a bachelor who had been forced to give up the priesthood through ill health. Some wagons were loaded here, mainly timber traffic, and stone from Banavie Quarry, some of which was used for foundation

Below:
The 17.40 Mallaig-Fort William prepares to depart behind 'B1' 4-6-0 No 61401, which, according to the bufferbeam, is based at Thornton. The building behind the tender is the railwayman's hostel. *G. H. Robin*

Left:
Maude digs in to the climb to Glenfinnan,
28 May 1984. *Author*

Above:
**No 44767 works the first public steam service of
the 1985 season over Glenfinnan viaduct on
21 May 1985.** *Author*

Right:
**No 5305 heads one of the winter 1989 crew
training runs over Loch Nan Uamh viaduct on
1 December 1989.** *Author*

work for the construction of the Forth Road Bridge.

The stationmaster at Banavie was provided with a motorcycle to enable him to visit those locations under his control, which included Locheilside, Corpach, Banavie Pier and of course Banavie itself. The swing bridge across the Caledonian Canal was the main feature. A boat – and there were passenger ships on the canal at that time – could take up to two hours to negotiate the flight of locks known as 'Neptune's staircase'. The swing bridge still functions as one of very few moveable bridges surviving in Britain today. Although now power worked, in the 1950s manual operation was the order of the day. There were two 'wheels' (similar to those found in signalboxes to operate conventional level crossing gates, but larger) to be swung. Two men were required, such was the weight of the bridge. The first wheel required rotating 180 times to raise the bridge onto the pivot, whilst the second carried out the actual turning operation. In a strong wind, a third man would be needed to assist. Naturally, staff were not over keen to turn 160 tons of bridge more often than necessary, and if there was no train due for a few hours the temptation to

Above left:
'J37' 0-6-0s Nos 64636 and 64592 are turned at Mallaig after arrival with the 'Jacobite' railtour, 1 June 1963. *Douglas Hume*

Left:
The 'Jacobite' railtour leaves Arisaig for Mallaig behind 'J37s' Nos 64592 and 64636, 1 June 1963. *Gavin Morrison*

Below:
North British Type 2 (Class 29) diesel-electric No D6133 heads the 17.35 Mallaig-Fort William near Arisaig, 24 August 1968. *C. Lofthus*

Left:
A scene typical of the 1970s – Class 27 No 27028 heads a Mallaig-bound train towards Glenfinnan.
Eric Aitchison

leave the bridge open was strong. Needless to say, occasionally they were caught out. The effect of a warm sun could increase the length of the bridge by up to an inch, meaning that it wouldn't close again. More than once staff at Banavie had the 13.30 down passenger whistling at the home signal whilst as many hosepipes as possible were deployed on to the bridge in an effort to cool it down, resulting in delay to the train and subsequent 'please explains' to the stationmaster. Even today the bridge sticking open is not unknown.

Banavie was another example of the community spirit which existed, often at the expense of railway regulations. Canal workers would often help out if extra staff were needed to swing the bridge on a windy day, or to cool it down if the worst happened. Banavie signalbox, located alongside the canal, became an unofficial meeting place between railway and canal staff, and the effect on working relationships would have been severe if Authority had decided to evict those not on official business.

The signalmen at Banavie had a profitable sideline breeding Cairn terriers, the chief sales outlet being the 'yuppy' element passing on the canal in fancy yachts, with wives/girlfriends becoming entranced with the puppies playing on the bankside.

The warmth and generosity of the people of Lochaber is illustrated by the experience of one newly appointed stationmaster, whose arrival had been delayed six weeks due to illness. His appointed residence – the station house at Banavie Pier, had lain damp and empty during this period. Arriving by train at Banavie to take up residence, he was surprised to be met by a local couple who insisted that the stationmaster and his wife should lodge with them until such time as the station house was properly warmed, aired and furnished, and subsequently refused all payment.

One morning the Banavie stationmaster received a 'phone call from Big Callum, a porter at Mallaig who had been a Japanese POW during the war. 'Are ye wantin' a fry, Willie?' Unloaded off the one o'clock was a crate containing seven stone of fresh herring. In the absence of any means of refrigeration it was duly distributed to the staff and residents in the area. The next day the stationmaster was confronted by a furious local fishmonger, who had been unable to sell any fish all day!

The railway, with its staff and equipment, provided an efficient transport and communication system for the various illegal poaching activities that went on. To quote just one example, on one occasion a guard who was a well known local poacher had been out on Loch Eil and had caught 40 or so good sea trout. He had left his catch in a surfacemen's bothy (hut) to be picked up later by the stationmaster with his motorbike. If the guard had been challenged, he would have been caught rowing an empty dinghy. The stationmaster, as a respected member of the community, was of course beyond suspicion.

Competition for the annual best-kept station garden competition was strong. Banavie was in a good position for growing, being nearly at sea level, but was overrun with rabbits. The stationmaster kept a 12-bore handy to deal with the problem. The signalman could see clearly down the platform and if he saw a rabbit he would give the SM a tinkle on the circuit phone. 'Ay, Willie, there's a rabbit eatin' ya carnations.' A barrel would then be let off at the offending animal. Fortunately no passengers got in the way. On another occasion a prize bull had been offloaded unexpectedly from one of the mixed trains, and was tied up on the platform for a couple of hours awaiting collection. During this period it proved to be an efficient deterrent to potential customers.

Glenfinnan station boasted one of the great sources of West Highland folklore, John Monaghan, who was stationmaster there for the best part of 35 years. He came from a railway family and had a brother in Glasgow's Queen Street Control office. John was basically a likeable rogue, and his reputation spread the length of the West Highland to Glasgow and beyond. In common with several other West Highland stations, Glenfinnan was also the local post office and John doubled as stationmaster and postmaster. To finance various peripheral activities, John was in the habit of borrowing from one till to make up for deficiencies in the other. Needless to say, he lived in fear of a visit from an auditor from either stable. The highly efficient West Highland grapevine which existed assured that the identity of any stranger, or 'hat', was wired forward as soon as the visitor had passed Craigendoran Junction, gave John ample time to prepare his defences, which consisted of lavish West Highland hospitality presented in such a manner that objections or refusals were simply cast aside as irrelevant. Upon arrival at Glenfinnan, the auditor or HQ representative was led down to the station cottage, introduced to Mrs Monaghan and given an extremely large 'dram' which was quickly replenished once the glass was empty. This was followed by a positively enormous lunch consisting of fresh local produce cooked to perfection by Mrs Monaghan, washed down with plenty more 'drams'. It logically followed that any form of concentration during the afternoon was simply not possible, and the visitor found that it took all the will power that he could muster to stagger on to the next southbound train and thankfully drift into slumber. There remained the problem of what to do if both Railway and Post Office auditors arrived on the same day, but as far as we know this never happened.

One day an officer's special full of inspectors, top brass and fat controllers was due from Glasgow on an official visit. Rather surprisingly it was running almost an hour early. John had accepted the train from Camus-Na-Ha but had then paid a brief visit to the nearby Stage House Inn, where he was delayed on an 'important business matter'. To his horror, he heard the special whistling furiously at the home signal. John finished his 'dram' and rushed up the embankment, stopping on the way to scoop several handfuls of cow dung about his person. He also scooped more dung around the line, before hurrying to the signalbox to admit the special to the station. The Senior Managers on the train were greeted by a breathless, dung-covered stationmaster panting 'Sorry about that, Sir,

Below:

No 2005 leaves Arisaig for Mallaig with the 'Royal Scotsman' on 28 October 1987. *Eric Aitchison*

Right:

Against stormy skies, the 'Royal Scotsman' crosses Glenfinnan viaduct on the return trip, 28 October 1987. *Roger Hill*

I had to chase cattle of the line!' Although no doubt suspicious, there was little that could be said or done in the face of the evidence.

John never had to buy coal for his own use. He kept a wheelbarrow alongside the water column and enginemen would fill the barrow with coal while taking water. John would chat to locomen while this was being done and would set down the Lochailort-Glenfinnan token on the loco tender and forget to retrieve it when the train moved off towards Fort William. This would mean a frantic 'phone call to the stationmaster at Banavie.

'That You, Willie?'

'Ay.'

'Is your motorbike handy?'

'Ay.'

'That Effin engine driver's away with two tablets again!'

The Banavie stationmaster would then try to intercept the train at Locheilside or Corpach, retrieve the token and return it by road to Glenfinnan, where it would be inserted in the token machine. Only then could the Lochailort-Glenfinnan section be cleared. Normally the Mallaig line 'team spirit' could be relied upon to hush the matter up, but there was at least one occasion when John was 'shopped' by a driver who found himself in mid-section with two tokens.

The unofficial distribution of locomotive coal to lineside houses was commonplace, and a well-intentioned head office scheme to lay on a special coal train when needed to distribute domestic coal was greeted with dismay by those living near the line, as now they would have to pay for their coal instead of getting it free off passing locomotives, even though the coal was supplied at discount rates. John was able to top-up his beer money by selling this extra supply locally, so he had no objections.

Another unofficial practice was that last thing at night a token would be taken out of the machine at Lochailort for the first up train the following morning, and the signals cleared at Glenfinnan. This way John got a lie in every morning. Of course one morning the inevitable happened – he had forgotten to clear the home signal, and woke up to the sound of the 06.30 mixed whistling furiously for the road.

The sight of Mr Monaghan in his stationmaster's hat and jacket over his pyjamas, climing up the bank from his cottage to the lineside and clearing the home signal by the simple expedient of pulling the wire up from its pulleys, will be recounted by Mallaig line drivers to their colleagues and children for many years to come.

John's main sideline (he had many) was the secret training of Greyhounds, which were subsequently introduced to Glasgow racetracks by his brother Frank, who moved in the appropriate 'circles'. On one occasion one of the dogs ran off with a token into the countryside, where it remains buried somewhere to this day.

On another occasion one of the dogs escaped from Glenfinnan platform whilst waiting to be loaded into the van of a Glasgow-bound train. John is alleged to have shouted at a waiting passenger, 'Stop that dog – it's a parcel!' The dogs were fed on herring, and one attempt to remove a few fish from a van in Glenfinnan station resulted in several hundredweight of fish on the platform and the track. On another occasion John left his hat in one of the fish vans, but unfortunately we don't know whether he ever got it back.

John worked shift and shift about with the Glenfinnan signalman, a common arrangement on the West Highland. There was no love lost between the two men, and the signalman wrote to the district office in Glasgow stating that Monaghan had arranged for railway-owned trees on the station approach to be felled, and subsequently sold at £25 each. 'Ay, he's right,' Monaghan is alleged to have said, 'but I didn't get £25 each, I got £65 each!' He got away with it yet again, by claiming that the trees had shielded sunlight from his cottage, and that the resulting dampness had made his wife ill. No more was heard of the incident.

Below:
The Banavie Swing Bridge is little changed in appearance. The fireman of No 5407 is about to surrender the token, 4 September 1985.
Stephen Robinson

tions were unmanned, but the locomotive slipped quietly through without a token. One or two sets of points were run through as a result, but these were quickly and quietly put right by the S&T department the following morning.

An English tourist was strolling through Morar village one day and across the level crossing. He noticed that one of the gates was not properly closed, and was lying half-open. This was due to irregularities in the road surface preventing the gate being pushed fully home. The tourist asked the crossing keeper, who was standing nearby, why the gates were half open. 'Simple,' replied the crossing keeper. 'I'm only half expecting a train!'

Most of the events described in the preceding two chapters took place in the late 1950s, and there is absolutely no doubt that in the foregoing I have but scratched the surface of the vast fund of railway folklore that exists around the Mallaig extension.

Other sidelines included a camping coach, which, when not let out by the appropriate department, was let locally by John, with proceeds going you-know-where! He also let out his own house to summer visitors, with himself and his wife sleeping on camp-beds in the booking office. He was also known to have let space in the signalbox for hikers to bed down, for an appropriate renumeration of course.

After retirement from railway service, John moved to a bungalow in Glenfinnan, and continued to manage the local post office. He died in an Inverness mental hospital, and the West Highland lost one of its most popular characters.

Another striking example of the community spirit that existed occured one night when the wife of a Mallaig driver became seriously ill, and required urgent medical attention in hospital in Fort William. An engine with steam and a coach was hastily put together and set off in the wee small hours for Fort William with the patient on board. All the sta-

Top left:
To work Fort William-Mallaig, steam has also operated trains south of Fort William: 'K1' No 2005 blasts away from Bridge of Orchy with a Fort William-Glasgow railtour on 15 November 1987. *Author*

Top right:
No 5305 heads towards the famous horseshoe curve with the VIP special from Fort William to Crianlarich on 23 October 1989, which was run to commemorate the cutting of the first sod in the line's construction one century previously. *Author*

Above:
No 5305 heads an LCGB special up Beasdale Bank, 2 September 1989. *Roger Hill*

Left:
No 37401 heads the 10.05 Fort William-Mallaig alongside Loch Dubh, 28 May 1986. *Author*

Return to Steam

Opinion differs widely as to who can take the credit for the brainwave that has since become BR's most successful regular steam operation. BR drivers at Mallaig insist the idea was theirs; Fort William's current ScotRail manager states with authority that the original notion came from one of his predecessors. Another BR source – closely connected with the introduction of the steam service – is equally adamant that the idea originated from a leading member of the steam preservation movement from south of the border.

The true origin of the reincarnation of steam probably lies somewhere in between, with the factors mentioned above contributing to the final decision. Colin Shearer, BR's Area Manager at Fort William at the time, remembers the period well. 'The idea was a collective one,' he recalls, 'coming through the Area Business Group.' (This group of area managers, engineers and local community members met regularly to discuss train services and opportunities for improvement.)

'The idea was essentially the right idea at the right time,' Colin continues, 'coming in the short period when area managers had business responsibilities, before the advent of the business sectors in their present form. We'd already tried many marketing initiatives – the Mallaig line Sunday service, and observation cars for example. Steam traction was the logical next step.'

What is beyond doubt is that the steam renaissance would not have happened without the support and backing from Chris Green, newly appointed Scottish Region General Manager, and his Regional Operations Manager Viv Chadwick, who was an ex-steam fireman, and knew what was involved in running and maintaining steam locomotives. Local opinion was that the branch to Mallaig, a remote, almost forgotten outpost of British Railways Scottish Region (Chris Green's ScotRail was in its infancy) was doomed to closure sooner or later. The

Right:
'. . . For those fortunate enough to be there, the sight and sound of the 96-year-old locomotive, slowed to walking pace by the gradient, beautifully backlit with her exhaust slamming vertically into the still spring air, will never be forgotten . . .' *Maude*, **28 May 1984.** *Author*

Left:
**Running two hours late thanks to *Maude's*
problems earlier in the day, No 5407 climbs away
from Glenfinnan on 28 May 1984 with the first BR
public steam service to Mallaig since 1963.
Bridge 70 is a typical example of the use of
concrete for engineering structures by the line's
engineer Sir Robert McAlpine.**
Author

As well as the 'Black Five' hauled
trains, it was proposed to run a Fort
William-Glenfinnan service with two
coaches only, to see if there was a market
for shorter steam journeys with historic
locomotives. The SRPS's own 'J36' 0-6-0
Maude was chosen for this task.

Steam returned to the Mallaig line on
Thursday 24 May 1984, after an absence
of over 20 years. Manchester businessman Paddy Smith's 'Black Five' No 5407
took four coaches of invited guests and
media representatives to Mallaig. Apart
from some slight difficulty ascending the
1 in 48 Beasdale Bank, all went well. On
arrival at Mallaig, there was a short ceremony when keys for the former Railwayman's Hostel at Mallaig were handed
over to the Community Council, as the
building was earmarked for a museum
project (an abortive one as things turned

Below:
**No 5407 heads the second of the day's two LCGB
excursions from Fort Wiliam to Mallaig, passing
the head of Loch Shiel between Glenfinnan
viaduct and Glenfinnan station. This picture
typifies the magnificent vistas which constantly
appear to delight the traveller, 27 May 1984.**
Author

plan to reintroduce steam was therefore
welcomed by most staff and by the local
community.

But not all the credit should go BR's
way – were it not for the sterling efforts
of SLOA and the steam locomotive owners, who had the job of providing volun-
teer labour to ensure their locomotives
were ready for the road, fed and watered,
with a full head of steam when required.

Stuart Sellar, leading SRPS member and
BR manager based in Glasgow was
seconded to the post of 'Project Manager,
Fort William Steam', and had the daunt-
ing task of planning, marketing, publicis-
ing and assisting in the introduction and
initial operation of the steam service.
One of Stuart and Colin's first tasks was
to ensure that there were sufficient
drivers at Fort William prepared to volun-
teer for steam duties. During initial staff
consultation, it is not surprising that one
of the chief worries of the staff was that
the steam service was the first step in selling off the railway into private hands.
These fears had to be put aside; steam
was only intended to provide contributory revenue towards that from the line
as a whole.

Coal supplies were a major headache,
thanks to the antics of one A. Scargill
Esq. Fortunately, the coal merchant con-
veniently located within Fort William
Goods Yard was able to obtain suitable
coal from Poland and France for the first
season of operation. There were also worries about the footplate crew's willingness
to use imported coal in view of the stated
policy of their trade union towards the
national coal dispute. Fortunately common sense won the day. The original
steam service was not planned to operate

every day of the week, due largely to the
availability of steam trained crews, bear-
ing in mind the need to provide relief to
cover holidays and sickness. Suitable
overalls for locomen were fortuitously
obtained cheaply from a YTS project in
Fort William.

Fire risk was, and still is, a problem
area, despite the fact that this area of
Western Scotland has high rainfall fig-
ures. At first, local landowners were
vigorously opposed to the scheme, and
BR was publicly accused of acting irre-
sponsibly. Much work had to be done to
alter this opinion. Lineside vegetation
had increased considerably since the
cessation of regular steam operations,
and this was to prove troublesome when
the steam service started.

Weight restrictions dictated the initial
choice of motive power and although
'Black Fives' never ran to Mallaig in the
days of steam (they were the mainstay of
Fort William-Glasgow services), the pro-
fusion of active members of the class in
preservation which were available for BR
running, the familiarity of Fort William
crews with these engines and the willingness of loco owners to make their engines
available to a large extent determined the
initial choice of motive power.

Behind all the preparations were worries about passenger loadings. Would the
service attract custom? The ability for a
whole family to abandon the car and
enjoy a day out which included scenery
and an element of novelty and nostalgia
was seen the main selling point, with
organised sightseeing tours by coach as
the prime area of competition. The service had to cover its costs *and* contribute
revenue to survive.

Right:
'K4' No 3442 *The Great Marquess* near Glenfinnan, 25 July 1989. *Brian Dobbs*

Below:
No 5305 is silhouetted against a wintry sky with a return driver training trip, 7 December 1989. *Roger Hill*

Left:

No 44767 heads across the causeway at the Western End of Loch Eilt with the return Mallaig-Fort William train, 18 July 1984.

Dr W. A. Sharman

hastily manufactured at the SRPS depot in Falkirk and transported to Fort William, where it was found to be 1mm out in size. Wiggins Teape at the Corpach Pulp Mill came to the rescue by allowing the use of its workshop so that the offending part could be re-machined. The part was fitted to *Maude* which then spent the night running up and down the depot yard to bed the new strap in.

The following day dawned bright and clear – a remarkable enough event in the West Highlands without the added attraction of steam. At about 08.30 *Maude* left Fort William with four packed coaches, bound for Mallaig. She trundled along the first 13 or so miles alongside Loch Eil, and then dug into the climb to Glenfinnan. For those fortunate enough to be there, the sight and sound of the 96-year-old locomotive, slowed to walking place by the gradient, beautifully backlit with her exhaust slamming vertically into the still spring air will never be forgotten.

But although the spectacle represented steam at its aesthetic best, all good things have their drawbacks. In this case there were two. Firstly, *Maude's* laboured efforts had delayed the train – she was already half an hour down and more troubles were in store. Remember there was the normal train service to run as well as the steam specials. Secondly – and more seriously – No 673 demonstrated very successfully what a highly efficient machine a coal fired reciprocating steam locomotive is for setting the countryside on fire, leaving behind her a trail of fires which were tackled by residents, enthusiasts, forestry workers and, eventually, the fire brigade.

Maude had, by this time, reached Glenfinnan. The local operating manager had to decide whether, in view of late running and fire hazard, to allow the special to continue, or to insist on her returning to Fort William and risk the wrath of the train passengers and associated bad publicity resulting from things being curtailed on the inaugural weekend of steam. It was a nightmarish decision. In the event *Maude* had a drink and carried on her way, setting off more fires in the process. A delay not bargained for was the pause for several runpasts for tour passengers at Lochailort. Although again

out). Initial publicity was given a fillip when the event made the national television news.

After the initial VIP/Press special, steam got down to business the following weekend, with two return trips with 5407 as part of an LCGB railtour on the Sunday, followed by a run with the veteran *Maude* to Mallaig on the Monday morning, with the first of the BR runs in the afternoon. It was a holiday Monday in England but not in Fort William. The Sunday trips went off without incident, though there were three or four unofficial runpasts as 5407 lost her feet on the short sharp climb from Glenfinnan Viaduct to the station, much to the amusement of the multitude of foreign tourists watching from the visitor centre, many of whom obviously thought BR still ran steam.

The bad news was that on arrival at Fort William, *Maude* was found to have a broken eccentric strap. A new part was

Left:

No 44767 heads a special McAlpine's charter towards Glenfinnan station on 2 October 1984. This is one of the very few special trains which have utilised coaches other than the Fort William-based steam set (other than the regular cruise trains). This train has a Mk II BSK, a kitchen car, and three Metro-Cammell pullmans which belong to SLOA. *David Eatwell*

running short of water, *Maude* had no option but to plod on to Arisaig. She never did make Mallaig by herself, though she did get there later that year coupled to No 44767. At Arisaig, once the following service train had passed on its way to Mallaig, a prompt run round took place, followed by a tender first run to Loch Dubh (Black Loch) where a hose was dropped into the loch for much needed refreshment, or at least that was the plan. But the pump refused to function and the footplate crew were faced with the prospect of slinging out the fire (onto tinder-dry countryside) and sending for assistance – the nearest diesel was at Fort William.

Legend has it that BR's InterCity charter manager – who was travelling on the train – set off with the single line token to try to commandeer a passing tourist who would take him by car to Glenfinnan to admit an assisting locomotive to the section.

Meanwhile, all was not well off the footplate. One of the fires had burnt through the telegraph wires (removed since the advent of RETB) and a token failure had resulted. As far as the operating authorities were concerned, *Maude* was effectively lost in section between Arisaig and Glenfinnan. The afternoon BR steam trip with 5407 was already sitting in Glenfinnan Down Platform. Colin Shearer set off by car to find *Maude*, stopping on the way to help put out a few fires.

Maude's pump had, by now, sprung into life, the tender was replenished and she set off on her way again, stopping for a blow-up on the 1 in 50/1 in 48 climb alongside the southern shore of Loch Eilt. Eventually she reached Glenfinnan, where 5407 had been waiting for almost two hours. There were two steam-hauled

trains in the tiny station. What was left of the West Highland's public timetable was in tatters. The afternoon Euston sleeping car express left Fort William extremely late, the special to Glasgow and points south was even later, around four hours, if I recall. Colin drove back to his office in a state of exhaustion. He answered the phone. It was Chris Green in Glasgow. Colin braced himself for what was to follow – stop playing steam trains immediately and run the service! Instead, Colin received Chris Green's congratulations on the successful inauguration of the steam service! The 'GM' could see beyond a few teething problems.

But the lessons had been learnt. The steam service must run reliably if it was

to succeed. Those mysterious forces of nature which conspire to ensure that what would be manageable delay on a 'normal' railway is multiplied by a factor of 5 on the West Highland had manifested themselves again. Although there was plenty of demand for special trains, it paid not to attempt the over-ambitious. The first few weeks of the public service were in fact run with four coaches only, so as to assess accurately the capabilities of the locos and due to the continuing uncertainty over coal supplies. Business was being turned away to ensure reliability.

Fire prevention arrangements, too, were put on a proper footing. A conference between Colin or one of his team and the local landowners took place each morning which identified any high risk areas, and arrangements were made to provide staff who would be on hand to deal with any outbreaks. Vegetation was cut back, ditches were dug in certain places, and locomotives were fitted with spark arresting devices. Even so, there have been occasions when cancellation or diesel substitution has been the only safe option.

On the plus side, the service was selling itself. The sight of a 'Five' steaming through Lochaber is too much to resist, and Colin was faced with queues in Fort William booking office. The shorter trips to Glenfinnan with *Maude* did not sell so well and were abandoned after the first year.

As I have mentioned, there was demand for special trains. At least one pop video has been filmed on the line, and a BBC TV special programme featuring Scottish singing star Barbara Dickson came over very well. One weekly special train to run has been the 'Royal Scotsman' luxury cruise train, which features a week long tour around Scotland, featuring steam between Fort William and Mallaig. A second cruise train, the rival 'Queen of Scots', ran only in 1990. The other 'regular' special workings have been BR's 'West Highlander' weekend excur-

sions from London, but these now use diesel haulage to keep costs down, and to avoid the need to provide an 'ETHEL' to heat the train.

After the first year's operation Colin and Stuart had the satisfaction of seeing the revenue graph in Colin's office show a marked increase over the previous, non-steam, year. Since then steam operations have settled down to a regular pattern which works. Although publicity, etc, is now handled by 'head office' there is little doubt that the service sells itself, both by word of mouth and because it is its own moving advertisement. Further welcome publicity came from a BBC TV programme in the 'Steam Days' series. As reported in the national press at the time, BR's most recent initiative has been to ensure sufficient footplate crews are available for future steam operation by running four weeks of special steam training runs in November and early December 1989, using No 5305 and five coaches brought out of storage at Perth. Unfortunately it wasn't possible to run these

Above:
'K1' No 2005 storms up Beasdale Bank, August 1987. The origin of the appropriate headboard is unrecorded. *Brian Dobbs*

Right:
'K4' No 3442 *The Great Marquess* makes a triumphant return to the West Highland. Beasdale Bank, 25 July 1989. *Tony Woof*

trains for passengers but photographers were treated to some magnificent smokescapes in the winter light. The training means three more trained drivers are available, which is very necessary as the more senior drivers approach retirement.

The novelty value of BR training drivers to handle steam locomotives was picked up by several national newspapers and television news programmes.

One of the most remarkable aspects of the Fort William-Mallaig steam operation has been the authenticity of locomotives used. The following chapter details the preserved engines which have appeared on the line since 1984 together with some historical details of each one. Each class of locomotive could be seen in and around Fort William in the days of steam, and, with the exception of the 'Fives', regularly worked the Mallaig extension. Furthermore, 'K1s' and 'K4s' were built specifically with the West Highland lines in mind, and No 3442 was of course a regular West Highland engine.

There is no doubt that the ability to hire a loco to BR for a West Highland sea-

son brings welcome revenue for loco upkeep, plus more than its fair share of headaches, principally those of providing support crews and high levels of wear and tear caused by locos spending 50% of their time in traffic running tender first.

Generally, there is no shortage of volunteers prepared to undertake the many unseen and unglamorous tasks necessary to prepare a locomotive for the road, and to put it to bed again afterwards. However, finding people with time to spare midweek who are prepared to travel the long distances involved is another matter. Steve McColl has acted as a solo support crew member for No 44932. 'You get absolutely exhausted and utterly filthy. The "Royal Scotsman" is the worst turn. An 08.30 departure (the train has since been retimed later) means getting up at four. What's worse is the Americans on the train don't even look at the engine. But everyone at Fort William makes us welcome. I found a parcel of fresh salmon in my bag when I was on the way home.'

Tender-first running is another matter. For a start, it's thoroughly unpopular with loco crews, as the weather can blow straight into the cab, and involves driving at an awkward angle in order to get a clear view of the road ahead. Loco owners don't like it as the engines are simply not designed to run tender-first for long periods. Excessive wheel flange wear is the main problem encountered. At one time it seemed likely that a turntable would be installed at Mallaig. This, together with a new triangle laid at Fort William primarily to allow the civil engineer to turn his track maintenance machines, would have eliminated the problem. But for various reasons both projects have floundered, and it now looks as though tender-first running will be with us for the foreseeable future.

Due to an error in early 1985, No 5407 arrived at Fort William with her smokebox facing east. She ran like this for a week or two, to the delight of photographers who made the most of the opportunities presented. However, the periodic statutory inspection which required the engine to be placed over the pit was not possible with the loco in this position so arrangements had to be made to turn her. Unfortunately for the cameramen, great care has been taken to ensure that steam locos arrive at Fort William with smokebox facing towards Mallaig ever since.

In 1987 the 'Fives' monopoly was broken by the welcome appearance of NELPG's 'K1' 2-6-0 No 2005. She quickly proved herself equal to the task required of her, once the firemen had acquainted themselves with the nuances of her firehole door. She returned for a second season in 1988, and a third in 1990.

Preserved Steam Locomotives

This chapter looks at the histories of the various locomotives which have escaped the cutter's torch and made it into the preservation world, and have subsequently appeared on Mallaig line steam workings.

1984, the first year of steam working, saw Class 'C' 0-6-0 ('J36') *Maude* in the company of two LMS 'Black Fives' Nos 5407 and 44767.

No 673 *Maude's* adventures on the West Highland in May 1984 are described elswhere. The class was associated with the line since its opening, surviving on Fort William pilot working until the end of regular steam in 1963. No 673 emerged from Neilsons of Springburn, Glasgow in 1891. She had 167 sisters, all built to a design of the NBR's locomotive engineer Matthew Holmes. Although intended for long-distance freight work, No 673 was fitted with the Westinghouse brake which enabled her to work passenger trains. The entire class was rebuilt in the 1920s by W. P. Reid, Homes's successor. A larger boiler and a full cab with side windows were the main differences. No 673 was so treated in 1915.

In 1917 she found herself being shipped to north-west France to work supply trains to the Western Front. She returned to Scotland in 1919, where 'she' was named after Lt-Gen Sir Frederick Maude who defeated the Turks in Mesopotamia in 1917. 25 'J36s' went to France for war service and all were named after war heroes.

She spent the rest of her working life at Haymarket shed in Edinburgh. She became LNER No 9673, later being renumbered to 5243, becoming 65243 after nationalisation. She was saved from scrap by the SRPS, and after a lengthy restoration was steamed again in 1978. Since then she has achieved notoriety, not only for her West Highland exploits but also by working under her own steam to and from BR's 'Rocket 150' celebrations on Merseyside in 1980, several steam

Above right
No fishing, but railway photography is fortunately permitted. No 5305 makes heavy weather of the climb past Loch Eilt, 31 August 1989. *Author*

Right:
No 44871 passes the tranquil white sands of Morar on her return trip from Mallaig, 6 August 1989. *Author*

excursions through Central Scotland, and a magnificent overnight solo run over the Highland Main Line from Perth to Aviemore, en route to ScotRail's Inverness Open Day in 1986. Following the expiry of her boiler certificate she has now retired to the SRPS's Bo'ness & Kinneil railway. Currently she is undergoing a complete overhaul, and it is hoped that she will one day turn a wheel on BR metals again.

'Black Five' No 5407 was born in 1937 at Armstrong Whitworth's, Newcastle. She soon lost her Geordie accent and, in common with the other 841 'Black Fives', spent the rest of her life doing unremarkable work in unremarkable places such as Shrewsbury, Derby, Holbeck, Saltley, Kentish Town, Nottingham and finally Lostock Hall. She achieved brief fame in February 1958, when, according to *Railway Magazine*, she topped 90mph between Luton and Bedford with a down Midland line express, in the hands of a Kettering crew.

Manchester businessman Paddy Smith bought No 5407 in 1975, running her on the mainline for four years as BR 45407. She made her public debut in LMS livery shuttling up and down the site of the 'Great Railway Exposition' at Manchester's Liverpool Road station in 1980.

No 44767 was a Crewe product of 1948, and although a thoroughbred 'Black Five', she is non-standard in that she is fitted with Stephenson Link Motion instead of the usual Walschearts valve gear. The vast majority of her working life was spent at Bank Hall shed, Liverpool, from where she worked Trans-Pennine expresses and other work on the ex-Lancashire and Yorkshire Railway system. She was withdrawn from Carlisle (Kingmoor) in 1968 and, according to (unsubstantiated) legend, was only saved from being turned into paper clips by the fact that the cutters had given up work for the day as they had run out of gas. She was purchased by businessman Ian Storey, and has made various sorties on to the BR network. She can usually be found hard at work on the steeply graded and spectacular North Yorkshire Moors railway. She was named *George Stephenson* after the famous railway engineer at the Stockton & Darlington 150th Anniversary celebrations at Shildon, Co Durham, in 1975.

Nos 5407 and 44767 both returned to Lochaber for a second season in 1985, and 44767 again in 1986, this time in the company of 44932, a Horwich product of 1945. No 44932 worked at various sheds

Above left:
'K4' No 3442 *The Great Marquess* crosses Loch Nan Uamh viaduct bound for Mallaig on 15 July 1989. *Brian Dobbs*

Left:
No 5305 pauses at Glenfinnan during one of the driver training runs, as Fort William driver Alec MacDonald looks down, 23 November 1989. *Author*

in the North West and East Midlands, namely Blackpool, Agecroft, Coalville, Nottingham, Cricklewood, Annesley, Rose Grove and Kingmoor, from where she was purchased in February 1969, then moving to Carnforth. She passed into her present ownership in 1983, and can normally be found on the Midland Railway Trust's line at Butterley, Derbyshire. Towards the end of the 1986 season No 44932's tyres were showing signs of excessive wear (a common West Highland problem) and the Humberside Locomotive Preservation Group's No 5305 was moved to Fort William later in the 1986 season. No 44932 will visit Mallaig again in 1991.

Since emerging from Armstrong Whitworth's Scotswood (Tyneside) works, No 5305 has spent time at Carnforth, Birkenhead, Edge Hill, Chester, Holyhead, Willesden, Crewe North, Crewe South, Springs Branch, Warrington and finally Lostock Hall sheds. She was bought for scrap by Mr A. E. Draper of Hull. Mr Draper's business had cut up 732 steam locomotives, but Mr Draper decided to save and restore 5305 as a memorial to the age of steam. 1984 saw No 5305 receiving the name *Alderman A. E. Draper*, and has returned to the Mallaig line in 1987, 1988, 1989 and 1990.

1987 and 1988 saw the 'Black Five' monopoly broken at last by 'K1' 2-6-0 No 2005. She is one of a numerous mixed-traffic design built as a result of Thompson's conversion of 'K4' No 3445 into the prototype 'K1/1'. She was built at Glasgow's Springburn Works in June 1949, and as such the number 2005 is inaccurate, for she was born into BR ownership as 62005 in BR lined black livery. She spent her entire career in the North East of England, principally at York and North Blyth depots. Although 'K1s' were regular West Highland performers, No 2005 is still regarded as a 'foreign' engine by Fort William crews, as she is fitted with a tender scoop for use with water troughs!

She was originally acquired for preservation by a syndicate comprising Lord Garnock, George Nissan, Brian Hollingsworth and Geoffrey Drury, and in 1972 was presented to the NELPG, one of the conditions of acceptance being that she be restored in her present LNER apple green livery. Restoration took place between 1972 and 1974, and has been hard at work on the North Yorkshire Moors Line, as well as occasional excursions onto the BR network (including three seasons at Fort William), ever since. At the time of writing she had clocked up 44,000 miles since preservation.

1989 saw two newcomers to the Mallaig steam service, though only one was new to the line. 'Black Five' No 44871, a 1945 Crewe product, arrived on the West Highland after a lengthy overhaul at Carnforth, under the eye of SRPS engineer John Allan. No 44871, once named *Sovereign* but now restored to the anonymity more in keeping with her

Above:
No 5305 is briefly illuminated near Loch Eil Outward Bound with a driver training run, 23 November 1989. *Author*

class, served at Bolton, Kingmoor, Carnforth, Crewe, Holyhead, Stockport, Trafford Park and Longsight, though not necessarily in that order. No 44871, although privately owned, is in the care of the SRPS on the Bo'ness & Kinneil railway. She is pencilled in for a further season at Fort William in 1991.

The other event of 1989 concerned Gresley 'K4' 2-6-0 No 3442 *The Great Marquess*. Her gradual restoration on the Severn Valley had been warranting attention from the BR powers-that-be for some time, as, being an ex-Eastfield engine with many Western Highland miles

Below:
No 5305 makes a stunning sight on the frosty morning of 1 December 1989 as it manoeuvres in Fort William's Mallaig Junction yard.
Stephen Robinson

under her belt, she was the obvious choice for the Mallaig steam service, both in terms of suitability for the job, and, as a genuine West Highland locomotive, as a crowd-puller. Indeed, the engine's owner, David, Earl of Lindsay, had expressed a strong desire to see No 3442 back on home ground.

Matters came to a head in April 1989 when David Lindsay became seriously ill. A fortnight's work for the engine on the West Highland was hastily arranged, though not without sterling efforts by BR and the SVR's support crew. In July 1989, No 3442 once again performed on the West Highland extension. On Saturday 15 July, a special train with 3442 in charge ran for the Earl of Lindsay, his family and friends. The Earl, weak with illness, managed a short footplate trip from Fort William to Banavie. He died just 16 days later, and the preservation movement, indeed railways generally, lost a great friend and ally.

Although No 3442 came briefly to Scotland again in 1990 as part of the Forth Bridge celebrations, she did not venture West of Haymarket. Nevertheless it is to be hoped that she will visit home territory again one day.

So what preserved engines might visit the West Highland in the future? Weight restrictions and curvature rule out all the main-line express classes. There is little doubt that 'Black Fives' will continue, if you'll excuse the pun, to 'hold the Fort'. A 'B1' is under restoration at Hull, which, if it were to visit Fort William, would continue the trend towards authenticity of locomotives used.

But one can always conjecture – a Standard 2-6-4T would be nice, or the Severn Valley's Standard Class 4 4-6-0 No 75069. Or what about one of the smaller ex-LMS 2-6-0s? Pity the large cylinders would probably exclude an ex-GW 'Manor'. . .

The Locomotive's Day

On Tuesday 7 September 1989, thanks to the co-operation of the SRPS and the owners of No 44871, I was able to join the support team in an effort to discover what went on out of the public eye which brings steam to life on a daily basis.

When I arrived at Fort William's Tom Na Faire Depot about 07.00 I found 44871 in steam with the support crew hard at work. Over a steaming mug of tea I asked 44871's custodian/engineer John Allan what time he had started. 'I've been at it all night,' was his reply. He'd been banking up the fire and generally keeping an eye on the engine, together with the rest of the four-strong support team, who

Below:
No 44871 receives lubrication prior to the day's work. SRPS engineer and 44871's custodian John Allan is on the left. *Author*

Below right:
The portable RETB unit mounted in No 44871's tender. *Author*

were based at Carnforth, 44871's home base, and were visiting Fort William to get acquainted with their steed. The last three hours work before the engine left the shed consisted of lubrication, keeping the fire in trim to ensure pressure up to the mark, a final water top up and of course a cosmetic rub down to keep the engine clean. In addition, water stand-pipes were dismantled and hoses rolled and stowed on the tender for use at Mallaig. There was an anxious moment when it was discovered that 44871 could not raise brake pipe vacuum much above 14-15in, compared with the 21in required to release the train's brakes, but it was found to be caused by the 'bag' (vacuum pipe) coming adrift from its dummy mount, which forms an airtight seal when the bag is not in use.

Shortly before 10.00 the BR crew arrived. Fort William's senior driver Neil MacRaild and fireman Brian Barbour were the rostered crew this week. The trip was a 'last' in two ways – it was 44871's last run of her 1989 (and only) season on

the Mallaig line, and it was also Fireman Barbour's last day in BR employment. Since BR's disposal of the Vale of Rheidol line, Brian must surely have been the only BR employee to spend his last day at work firing steam. Whilst it is sad to see young competent staff leaving railway service, promotion based on seniority means that Brian would have to leave Fort William in order to achieve driver status before early middle age.

Jokes and pleasantries were exchanged between the BR and support crews. The BR crew drive and fire, all other duties are the responsibility of the locomotive owner, though obviously a close working relationship is required whilst the engine is on BR metals.

Driver McRaild's first task was to check the radio module, which is mounted in the locker on 44871's tender and powered by two car batteries. The required contact with Banavie RETB Centre was made and the 'test token' obtained and displayed on the radio module. Until this is done, the locomotive is not permitted

Left:
Fireman Brian Barbour tends the fire before departure from Fort William, 7 September 1989. *Author*

which was quickly controlled by attention to the injectors. The required brake continuity test had been carried out. Douglas Hodgins, a leading SRPS member who organises 44871's support crews, appeared and requested smoke effects to be laid on leaving Banavie station and on Bleasdale Bank. A quick blast on 44871's whistle hustled the passengers onto the train, as the station starting signal changed from red to single yellow. Meanwhile driver MacRaild contacted Banavie again and was issued with a 'long section' token giving authority to proceed to Glenfinnan. The signalman's instructions were plainly audible despite the noise from the footplate. A few final rounds on the fire, a check that the starting signal was still 'off', and the guard gave the signal to start.

Driver MacRaild, with a skill born of many years of experience, got 44871 and her train on the move with only the briefest hint of a slip on the wet rails. The noise of 44871's exhaust penetrated the general roar of the footplate as we headed out of Fort William, past Mallaig Junction Yard and the depot and crossed the River Lochy. We paused alongside Banavie signalling centre to pick up a handful of additional passengers and for me to reflect on the strange paradox of a

to leave the depot. We climbed aboard and Driver MacRaild eased the regulator open enough for 44871 to move backwards towards the depot exit signal, which cleared as we approached. Although we were not booked to depart from the station for another 20min or so, the photographers were already out beside the line despite the rain. After a very brief pause, the 'calling on' signal allowed us into the occupied platform to back onto our seven coach train. A crowd

of intending passengers had gathered on the platform to greet us with enthusiasm. Brian raked and trimmed the fire, before stoking up to bring boiler pressure up to 225psi before departure. I stepped on to the platform and wondered why a black steam locomotive always looked so totally superb in wet weather, which always amplified the amount of smoke and steam.

The multitude of admirers on the platform were startled by 44871 blowing off,

Below:
Driver's eye view back along the train as No 5407 climbs above Loch Eilt on the return trip, 8th September 1985. *Stephen Robinson*

creation of the age of steam standing alongside a high-tech signalling installation. We caught sight of Douglas Hodgins and Roger Hill just beyond the swing bridge, and a few rounds on the fire earned us a thumbs-up sign as we pulled away. Once over the automatic open level crossing at Corpach and past the Corpach pulp mill, with the line's last semaphore signals protecting the level crossing giving road access to the pulp mill, we cruised alongside Loch Eil and past the Outward Bound school and its station. Despite the weather, lineside cameramen were out in force, and our crew derived considerable amusement from watching motorists on the adjacent A830 trying to drive and watch the train at the same time.

We passed a lineside cottage with much whistling, which was apparently a signal to the occupant that we were passed and she could now hang her washing out in safety. A repeat performance at another cottage near Locheilside was acknowledged by a wave from a lady at one of the windows. Later I learnt that this was Driver MacRaild's mother-in-law.

The end of Loch Eil was passed and Brian fed the fire. Pressure was 225psi as we hit the gradient, and 44871 was barking and slowing noticeably as the 1 in 48 bit. Despite her task, pressure remained steady and the safety valves lifted we entered the short tunnel through a rocky outcrop. The resulting cacophony in the cab was to cause me temporary deafness

for two days. We reached the summit of the climb and steam was shut off, and a gentle brake application made to check our speed as we descended round the sharp reverse curves and on to the viaduct. I felt immensely privileged to enjoy the timeless vista of the Glenfinnan Monument and Loch Sheil from the viewpoint of the cab, despite the wet weather. After the viaduct we blasted up the short but vicious 1 in 50 to the station, Driver MacRaild letting the gradient reduce our speed so that only the slightest brake application was needed to bring the train to a stand in Glenfinnan's down platform.

The up platform was occupied by main line liveried No 37406 on a ballast working, which was effectively shut in by No 44871 and her seven coaches. After returning the Fort William-Glenfinnan token, we were authorised by Banavie by radio to draw forward so that the rear of the train was clear of the loop points, allowing the ballast train to depart. This move duly took place. Further contact with Banavie then became hampered by noise and reception difficulties. We were required to wait at Glenfinnan to cross the late 10.35 'Sprinter' from Mallaig. We set back into the station to clear the West end points so that the Sprinter could run

into the loop. The delay was to cost about half an hour. We spent the time by chatting to some of the passengers, including a BR driver from Aberystwyth who had worked on the Vale of Rheidol.

An eerie squealing sound in the distance heralded the arrival of the Sprinter. Brian fed the fire for the steep climb away from the station and the passengers were ushered back on board. The Sprinter arrived, and the radio was coaxed back into life (it appeared that the battery should have been changed) for Banavie to transmit another 'long section' token, this time all the way to Mallaig.

The climb at 1 in 50 from a standing start is regarded by the footplate crews as being the toughest part of the run from both engine and driver. We had drizzle, a full load, an expert driver and plenty of steam. As the regulator was opened, 44871 slipped slightly and then recovered. The bark from the exhaust bounced back from the rock cutting walls as we moved steadily into the climb at 7-8mph. Despite her arduous task, Brian's firing kept 44871's pressure precisely at 225psi, and she started to blow off as we passed under the main road and into the glen. As we entered the curves 44871 lost her feet, to the consternation of the driver and the delight of the onlookers. The slip was quickly controlled but the performance was repeated six or seven times over the next 300yd or so, as we climbed alongside the river, which was swollen to a torrent by the rain. At last the gradient eased slightly and adhesion was regained.

Speed was difficult to estimate (for me anyway) as, like most other steam locomotives, 44871 is not fitted with a speedometer, but we were now soaring up the gradient. We must have looked a fine spectacle as a minibus load of Germans gave us a round of applause. We topped the climb, and Driver MacRaild shut off steam and made a brake application to bring speed down for the curves through the two short tunnels. The crew got a brief respite as we quickly dropped down the valley side until we were running alongside the Loch Eilt, for me the most beautiful stretch of the route. Driver MacRaild acknowledged a wave from fishermen in a small boat, and told me that they were probably Americans who have paid a four-figure sum to fish in one of Scotland's best salmon lochs.

We drifted across the short causeway at the Loch's western end, and then were climbing again alongside the road towards Lochailort. Beyond the station the fairly gentle climb continues through another short tunnel. The usual gathering of photographers greeted our appearance by the small chapel at Polnish. Speed increased as we coasted over the embankment at the east end of the 'Black Loch'. The regulator was opened again as we entered another short tunnel. I looked ahead over the driver's shoulder and we got the view of the line ahead. We were heading out of the tunnel and across the Loch Nan Uamh Viaduct and the dip

Below:
The natural amphitheatre which forms the setting for Glenfinnan Viaduct is seen to great effect in this view from the train headed by No 44767, 29 August 1984. *Stephen Robinson*

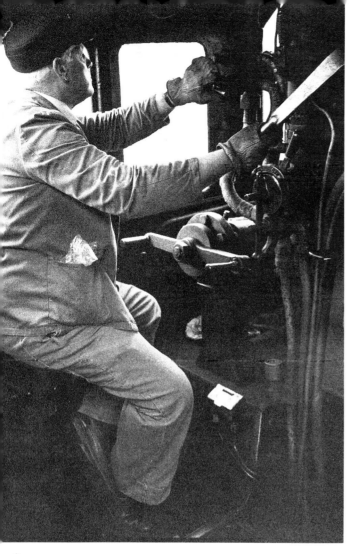

Above:
Fort William Driver Neil MacRaild at the controls of No 44871, 7 September 1984. *Author*

Above right:
No 44871 meets the late running 1025 Mallaig-Glasgow at Glenfinnan, 7 September 1989. *Author*

indicating the bottom of the 1 in 48 of Beasdale Bank was clearly visible. Speed must have been around 40mph but it felt much faster. The swaying and noise were unbelievable as we tore across the viaduct and into the first of the three tunnels. 871's staccato beat bounced back off the tunnel walls into the cab to assault the eardrums. All was activity on the footplate. Driver MacRaild concentrated on getting maximum tractive effort from 44871's full head of steam. Brian rhythmically fed the fire, making each shovelful count, and fiddled with the injectors to keep pressure high without blowing off. Our friend's request for smoke was not forgotten and extra rounds were shovelled furiously into the firebox, and as we entered the final tunnel the cab filled with smoke, steam, sound and fire. Despite the crew's efforts speed had dropped to what seemed to be about 20mph at the summit of the climb near Beasdale Halt. Waves were exchanged with passing motorists as steam was shut off and we drifted downgrade into Arisaig

station, where Brian took a well earned rest. Two small children on the platform, brought by their father to see the engine, sought comfort from him as 44871 blasted away on the final leg of the journey to Mallaig. The weather had now turned misty and the view out to sea was lost as we drifted across Keppoch Moss, where the line's engineers had resorted to the 'floating' technique to get the line across this bog on a bed of brushwood. This method of construction had also been used to get the West Highland line itself across Rannoch Moor, some 60 miles further south.

After slowing for the level crossing at Morar, we drifted back into Mallaig, where our BR crew left the train to take their meal break. While the loco was admired by the passengers, the support crew swung into action once more, setting up the standpipe and hoses to replenish 44871's tank. It seemed amazing that she looked so peaceful after her run, when only 15 minutes previously she had been tearing at Beasdale Bank like a demented dragon. All the accessible bearings were quickly lubricated before the BR crew reappeared to run the locomotive round the train and head back to Fort William.

I retired to the train to enjoy the scenery for the return to Fort William. The weather had improved somewhat, and the combination of the scenery with

the sound of smells of steam drifting in through the windows made it clear why this particular brand of nostalgia sells so well. A public address system, manned by SRPS volunteers, keeps passengers informed of the highlights of the route. The souvenir stall, situated in the brake compartment, is also run by the SRPS and is a useful source of funds for the society.

On arrival back at Fort William, once the passengers had disembarked, 44871 propelled the coaches back to the depot. The support crew started work again. The tender was topped up again, although, as this was 44871's last run of the season, the fire could be allowed to die down. Cleaning the fire and raking out the ashpan had to be done by crawling underneath the locomotive – not a pleasant task. Following this, the smokebox was emptied of soot by the simple but filthy expedient of shovelling it out by hand. Most of the support team were planning to return to Carnforth later that day, but John Allan would stay in Fort William as long as the locomotive was there, in order to carry out any necessary minor repairs and to simply keep an eye on things and, it must be said, to guard against any unauthorised interference.

Finally the time came to begin the trek south, and I regretfully tore myself away from the convivial atmosphere of the support coach after a most memorable day.

The Current Scene

Whilst there is no doubt that one of the prime attractions of the Mallaig line is its steam service, the main function of the route is to serve the transport needs of the area, and as such it forms a part of the national rail network. The many changes which have taken place both in the line's infrastructure, environment and motive power have tended to be overshadowed by steam operations. This chapter seeks to redress the balance.

The changes in the infrastructure of the line have been many and varied, the most dramatic of which was the closure of the original station at Fort William to make way for the new bypass road along the shore of Loch Linnhe. The present station, though uninspiring, is functional enough and is still convenient for the town centre. It opened on 13 June 1975. The line gained an additional station in 1985 with the opening of an unstaffed halt to serve the Outward Bound School at Loch Eil. It is situated between Corpach and Locheilside.

The introduction of radio signalling (RETB) has brought about considerable changes to the line's appearance, the most noticeable of which has been the removal of all semaphore signals, with the exception of those protecting the level crossing at Annat and in the vicinity of Fort William. As part of the conversion process, the whole of the West Highland system was worked on the electric token system for some months without lineside signals. This was achieved without difficulty or mishap, and raises the academic question of whether signals were ever required. Reflectorised boards have now replaced distant signals by the lineside where necessary. The classic latticework signal posts, so typical of the Scottish scene, remained until recently (minus arms) as silent reminders of the past, but most of these too have now been removed.

All trains are now controlled from Banavie signalling centre, which is situated next to the original Banavie signalbox. For a time during 1986 both boxes existed side by side. A style of architecture sympathetic to the design of the traditional building has been adopted for the new structure.

In 1985 the crossing gates at Morar, which had been operated by train crews for some years, were replaced by an automatic open crossing (AOCL) operated by the passage of trains. On 2 July 1985, the Royal Train conveying Their Royal Highnesses the Prince and Princess of Wales to Mallaig (for a visit to Skye) traversed the line behind spotless Class 37s Nos 37027 and 37011. After the Royal party had detrained, the locomotives ran round the train and were working the empty carriages back to Fort William when they struck a car on the newly installed Morar open crossing. The car was driven by an American tourist who claimed afterwards he didn't understand the meaning of the twin flashing red road signals, which, considering level crossings with similar protection arrangements are the norm in the US, is a bit much to expect us to swallow! Perhaps he was only half expecting a train! Fortunately damage to the locomotive was slight and the train was able to continue on its way with minimal delay.

Remote train control has dispensed with the need for station personnel to handle tokens and token equipment, and consequently all intermediate stations are now unstaffed. Fortunately, the common British vandal, who has scarred so much of the BR network, has not yet threatened the atmosphere of most of the stations. Former signal cabins at Mallaig and Arisaig are in use as store rooms for permanent way materials.

Due to changes within the fishing industry, and changes to the economics of freight transport by rail, fish traffic has all but vanished. The only freight traffic which remains is diesel fuel for the trawlers, and wagons of materials and stores needed by the engineer for maintraining the line. It was usually possible to move such wagons by simply attaching them to the rear of the passenger train, and indeed the 16.05 ex-Fort William was timetabled as a mixed until the introduction of Sprinters, thus carrying on a tradition which had been a feature of Mallaig line operation since its opening. It was common to see two or three oil tankers on the rear of a loco-hauled train, but other wagons were also conveyed. The author recalls sunbathing on Morar beach, having packed cameras away after the passage of the steam service. The 16.05 from Fort Wiliam then appeared with the usual Class 37, two

Below:
No 37412 'Loch Lomond' drops down to the shoreline of Loch Eilt with the 14.05 Fort William-Mallaig, 10 June 1988. *Gavin Morrison*

Above:
'Super Sprinter' unit No 156456, strengthened to three cars, skirts Loch Dubh with the 10.35 Mallaig-Glasgow, 27 July 1989. *Tony Woof*

Above right:
A three-car 'Super Sprinter' heads for Mallaig (away from camera) between the two short tunnels near the summit of the climb from Glenfinnan. A misty Loch Eilt can be seen in the background, 20 July 1989. *Author*

blue/grey coaches, two green/cream coaches and three assorted bogie vehicles containing permanent way bits and pieces!

A welcome return to freight traffic occurred in 1986 when a trawling company started to land red mullet at Mallaig. Although there is only a limited market for this fish in the UK it sells well in France, and Railfreight won a contract to convey it via Speedlink services and train ferries. The Italian 'Interfrigo' white vans made a fine sight against the Lochaber scenery, but their movement was unpredictable and were rarely caught by the camera. Regrettably the company involved went into liquidation and the freight resurgence lasted but a few months only. However the opportunites presented by the Channel Tunnel may, we can but hope, mean that traffic such as this could one day be seen again in the West Highlands.

1978 saw the introduction of the 1,750hp English Electric Class 37 diesels, the first and only diesel class with six-wheel bogies to appear on the line. These workhorses are still normally the only main line diesels to be seen, and the English Electric growl is now as synonymous with the West Highland as the bark

of a 'K2'. Since the demise of the '27s' in 1981, the only other diesels to appear have been the 1,000hp Class 20, normally confined to Fort William-Corpach trip freights but very occasionally substituting on passenger duty for a last minute '37' failure. The early 1980s saw Eastfield's fleet of '37s' for West Highland Working fitted with electric train heat equipment and numbered in the '374XX' series, but with a welcome return to 'Loch' names. May 1988 saw the RETB system brought into use, which meant that only radio-fitted '37s' from Eastfield can work the line. Since then the only visiting diesel locos have been an annual visit by a pair of Class 20s, now privately owned by Hunslet-Barclay and attached to the weedkilling train at either end.

That West Highland bugbear, excessive flange wear, reared its head on Class 37s, and a flange lubrication system was introduced on certain individual engines. However this system caused problems with track circuits when operating over conventional lines and was discontinued. In 1985 the Research Department conducted tests on the line which involved a Class 37 attached to one of their test coaches. The idea was to measure the behaviour of the bogies on sharp curves, and because the loco involved was attached to the test car by all manner of cables, running round was out of the question. Another loco was attached to the other end of the coach, and this strange combination made several trips over the line during the spring/early summer of 1985, stabling at Glenfinnan when not in use. As a result various modifications were incorporated into the Class 37 bogies to minimise flange wear.

Probably the greatest single revolution to affect motive power on the Mallaig line took place in January 1989 with the introduction of RETB-fitted Class 156 Super Sprinter diesel units based at Edinburgh's Haymarket depot. This influx of multiple units means that locomotives are only seen once or twice per week, either on the occasional ballast or trip freight, or on one of the 'West Highlander' land cruises from London.

Whether or not one takes to Sprinters is a matter of taste. On the plus side, they are comfortable and reliable, and the acceleration possible has meant a reduction in journey time. The reduced running costs in terms of maintenance, fuel consumption, number of locomotives required and wear and tear on the permanent way, will no doubt help to assure the future of the line. Similarly, the new timetable associated with the Sprinters has meant that two down and two up trains run through to Glasgow, with some services running through to Edinburgh. Mallaig line passengers probably now have their best ever timetable in terms of journey times and connectional possibilities.

The two main Sprinter-related problems have been capacity and 'squealing'. When one is accustomed to joining a six-coach summer loco-hauled Fort William-Mallaig train at Glenfinnan and being unable to find a seat (or, on occasions, somewhere to stand), it is not surprising to find that the Sprinter units are frequently overcrowded, and are unable to cope with large numbers of rucksack-equipped hikers en route to Skye. Some Class 156s have been re-marshalled into three-car formations in the summer months to help ease the problem.

The other problem which has occurred has been an unforeseen one – that of noise from contact between wheel flanges and check rails in the form of a high-pitched squealing sound which has brought complaint from both passengers and residents. The noise occurs on tight curves and is worst on dry days. In addition to the noise problem, ScotRail's engineers are experiencing heavy tyre wear, with turning being carried out more frequently than those which operate elsewhere on the network. This is not a new problem to WHL rolling stock!

The noise has been reduced to more acceptable limits by modifying the wheel – a thin sandwich of foam between the inside face of a light aluminium plate and the wheel web itself. Modifications are also in progress to cut down on flange wear problems.

In November 1990 the whole line was closed for 10 days. ScotRail's Civil Engineers removed the track from Glenfinnan viaduct and installed a modern waterproof membrane and improved drainage on the structure. The opportunity of 10 days without trains was taken to carry out repairs to the Swing Bridge at Banavie and to Borrodale Tunnel, as well as major track relays at Lochailort and Corpach.

Appendices

The Future

Mallaig has been transformed by the construction of the new A830 road along the shore, which has obliterated all traces of the former turntable and loco shed. Indeed the progressive improvement of the A830 will have a profound effect on this railway to the isles, as the projected route follows the railway closely. Not only, therefore, will road competition increase considerably, but the construction of the road may cruelly rob the railway of some of its scenic attractions. And if that were not enough, Her Majesty's Government have recently announced permission for a privately funded toll bridge from Kyle of Localsh to the Isle of Skye, which could have a serious if not devastating effect on the Mallaig-Skye ferry service, with knock-on effect on rail revenue.

However this is largely speculation as large parts of the A830 scheme and the Toll Bridge are still at the conceptual stage, with many hurdles of planning and bureaucracy to overcome. Would I be classed as a fuddy-duddy old reactionary if I said I hoped the plans got killed off? Is my attitude reminiscent of those who opposed the construction of the railway in the last years of the 19th century?

Even without these potential developments, the attitude of a government hell-bent on privatisation, the energy crisis, the prospect of the Channel Tunnel and the European Single market will all have their effect, one way or another, on what is, without a shadow of doubt, a highly agreeable stretch of railway. Let us hope that it will remain so.

The Glenfinnan Station Museum Project

The Glenfinnan Station Museum Trust is in the process of being set up to save a complete working West Highland station. This should ensure that at least one of the line's stations – arguably its most attractive one – survives destaffing and retains its pleasant atmosphere. The scheme involves the establishment of a museum and interpretive centre for the West Highland Railway (not just the Mallaig extension) in the station buildings with a reference library and reading room located in the former signalbox.

BR's reaction has been favourable, and a grant from the Railway Heritage Trust has enabled repair work to be carried out on the station buildings. The site will include a scenic viewpoint and a woodland walk, and will incorporate holiday accommodation which will hopefully, in the longer term, include a camping coach.

The project will demonstrate how an important listed building can be effectively reused to promote and encourage use of the rail line, particularly in association with local activity holidays and other visitor attractions.

A programme of 'working weekends' has already commenced, and further ones are planned to complete the formation of the Woodland Walk and viewing point, and to complete the restoration of the signalbox and reinstate the original signalling equipment, in non-working form.

It is hoped that the 1990 season will see progressive opening, with full opening in 1991.

The project is masterminded by John Barnes who can be contacted on Kinlocheil 295.

Further Reading

The following titles will provide many hours of enjoyable reading about the Fort William-Mallaig line and associated railways.

John Thomas; *The West Highland Railway;* David & Charles.
John Thomas and David Turnock; *A Regional History of the Railways of Great Britain Vol 15 – The North of Scotland;* David & Charles.
Neil Caplan; *Railway World Special – The West Highland Lines;* Ian Allan Ltd.
Alexander Frater; *Stopping Train Britain – A Railway Odyssey;* Hodder & Stoughton. This work first appeared as a series of articles in *The Observer* newspaper colour magazine, one of which features the West Highland.
Tom Noble; *The West Highland Mallaig Extension in BR Days;* OPC.
Tom Weir; *The Mallaig Line;* Framedram.
The Mallaig Railway – A guide to the line reprinted from the turn of the century, with modern illustrations; Famedram.
The Story of the West Highland – The 1940's LNER guide to the West Highland Railway reprinted; Famedram.

Viewing

You may enjoy these videotapes which feature the Mallaig line, though not necessarily as the main subject:

Steam to Mallaig – A Driver's Eye View; Video 125.
The West Highland Line; Video Highland.
Scottish Steam 1962-87; Transport Video Publishing.
Steam in the Highlands Nick Lera – Locomotion Productions.
Damned Good Time; Railfilms Ltd. This features *Maude's* spectacular run on 28 May 1984, as described in Chapter 4.
Paddy's Engine; Railfilms Ltd. Paddy Smith, the owner of 'Black Five' No 5407, tells his own story. Much Mallaig line footage.

Right:
The Royal Train conveying Their Royal Highnesses the Prince and Princess of Wales to Mallaig (for Skye) passes the chapel at Polnish, 2 July 1985. Nos 37027 and 37011 do the honours. *Dr W. A. Sharman*